RULES OF ENGAGEMENT

A GUIDE TO BETTER COMMUNICATION
AND BETTER RELATIONSHIPS
WITH EVERYONE WHO IS IMPORTANT
TO YOUR BUSINESS

ISBN 978-0-9823490-4-5

Dedicated to Chase & Maya (my kids) and my friends & co-workers at Olympus – such an amazing group of people, you inspire me daily. *Brian Adam*

As always, dedicated to my wife Lisa and Daughter Alix. This time, adding son-in-law Ross, and grandson Sidney Joseph Diamond. *Dave Fellman*

Cover Graphics Designed by Tim Kelly, timkelly@me.com, https://www.behance.net/TimKelly

Table of Contents

Introduction
Dave Fellman

Engage is an interesting word. You can engage in war, or in horseplay. You can engage a clutch, or a warp drive, You can be engaged to be married. In each application, the word means something different.

Think about the warp drive. Picture Jean Luc Picard, sitting in the Captain's Chair of the Enterprise. He gives the helmsman a course and speed and completes the command by raising his right arm, cocking his wrist forward and speaking one word: "Engage!"

Now let's stop for a moment. Most of you will get the reference. Some of you won't. And with those who don't, my attempt at engagement just failed. Here's a fundamental concept, engagement is all about communication, and real communication requires that both the sender and the receiver connect all the dots.

This is critically important, because it's possible to have 100% engagement even if you don't have 100% communication. I can be fully engaged and onboard with what I *think* you said, right? But that might take us anywhere between 1° and 180° off course. *Engagement is all about communication!*

This book is about engaging with everyone who is important to your business, inside and outside, which means employees, customers and even suppliers.

****

Here's another fundamental concept. Your business is all about selling something to somebody. That might sound a little mercenary, but please bear with me for a moment. It's true that many businesses seem to be more about buying than selling. A restaurant is a perfect example. Customers come in to buy a meal. There is *service* going on, but typically not a whole lot of *selling*. That's true of many other retail businesses.

But whether it's a laid-back level of service or a close-the-sale level of selling, the common factor is that *money changes hands* – although actually, that's only half of the story. Money goes one way, the product goes the other way. A trade occurs. A few thousand years ago, before the adoption of currency, all trading was product-for-product – or maybe more accurately, commodity-for-commodity. *I'll trade you one of my goats for a bushel of your wheat.* Or, *I'll trade you a days' worth of work for that bushel of wheat.* In modern commerce, it's far more likely to be product-or-commodity-for-currency. *I'll trade you one of my goats for $55,* or *I'll trade you an hour's worth of work for $18.55.*

At the most fundamental level, all business is transactional. At the highest level, though, I think we want it to be relational. That means customers who *want to* buy from us, employees who *want to* work for us, and even suppliers who really want to work *with* us. That's the goal of the sort of engagement this book is all about.

****

I'm a sales guy. I got my first sales job in 1978, selling restaurant equipment and supplies for a small company in Boston. I'd been working in restaurants for 6-8 years, including my college years, and I knew that I didn't want to do it anymore. My father, who was in sales most of his working life, encouraged me to try selling. So I did something I thought was pretty intelligent. I knew that I didn't know anything about selling, so I got a job selling something I knew something about. And I had some small successes, but overall, I'd have to call my year-and-a-half on that job a pretty complete failure. I got no training. I got very little support. And I didn't know how to compensate for all of that to build any sort of consistent results.

My Dad knew that I was struggling. He showed up at my apartment one Sunday morning with the Help Wanted section of the Boston Globe. He had circled one ad with a red Magic Marker, for a company called Moore Business Forms. "This is a good company," he told me. "They're a leader in their industry. If you can get this job, they'll train you and manage you and give you the kind of support you aren't getting now."

"I think you like selling," he continued. "I think you just need a better situation."

I sent in my resume, got called for an interview, got called back for a second interview, and ultimately got the job. And my father was right, they trained me and managed me and supported me and put me in position to succeed. Over the next five years, I got promoted from Sales Representative to District Sales Manager to a Divisional Staff position. And I learned that my father had actually understated my feelings about selling. I didn't just like selling, I loved it. But I have to draw an important distinction here. I don't love *sell*ing if the root word is used as a verb. I'm not one of those guys who gets off on making the sale. I do love *selling* when the whole word is used as a noun. My passion lies in understanding the dynamics of selling, and teaching others how to be successful at it.

Some of that may be because I'm not really a "people person." In fact, I'm a pretty classic introvert. Sure, I can interact with others, I do it all the time. But it depletes my battery – as opposed to classic extroverts who are energized by socialization and interaction. The common perception is that salespeople have to be outgoing. I guess I'm living proof that an introvert can still be successful in sales.

****

Brian Adam is a people person. I first met him in October 2018 when we were both on the program at SGIA Expo, a conference and trade show presented by the Specialty Graphics & Imaging Association. The program was titled Essential Small Business Strategies and Brian was the leadoff speaker. His topic was Engaging Your Employees. I was next, speaking on Launching A Strong Sales Effort.

As I listened to Brian, I was struck by the similarity in our message. He was talking about employees. I would be talking about customers. But we were both talking about *talking* – and not about talking *to* employees and customers, but rather about talking *with* them. Talking. Listening. Communication. Engagement!

Brian's whole philosophy seemed pretty straightforward. *If I build the kind of company that the best people will want to work for, we'll all be successful.* As a sales guy, I would only add this: *If you build the kind of company that the best customers will want to buy from, you'll be successful on both sides of The Point of Sale.*

1 The Point of Sale
Dave Fellman

The Merriam-Webster Dictionary defines "customer" as "one that purchases a commodity or service." The Business Dictionary (www.businessdictionary.com) adds another element to its definition: "A party that receives or consumes products (goods or services) *and has the ability to choose between different products and suppliers*."

The choosing element is very important to our discussion. From the selling side of the equation, I think it's critical to recognize the difference between customers and not-customers, and to reserve the term *customer* for people who are actually buying from you.

This is more than just semantics. Isn't it true that you engage differently with a neighbor as opposed to a stranger? You may not like your neighbor, but there's some level of familiarity and continuity in your relationship. The same is true with a person who has done business with you in the past. However, it's bad strategy to assume that same foundation with someone who hasn't.

I think there are actually four categories of people on the buying side of your selling equation. I call them suspects, prospects, customers and maximized customers. They are *suspects* when you have reason to think (or even hope) they might be prospects. They are *prospects* only when you know that they are qualified – more on that in just a moment. They become *customers* when they actually start buying from you. They (hopefully) become *maximized customers* when you're getting maximum value from the relationship.

Please note that I said *you're* getting maximum value from the relationship. It's well understood that a seller has to *provide* value. It's also well understood that a seller should value each customer – and make sure they know it! That's part of the whole *engagement* equation. But those two things only address one level of buyer-seller value, and I believe there are three levels. More on that too later on.

What does it mean to be a qualified prospect? At the very least, you have to know – not just think or hope! – that they buy, want or need whatever it is that you sell. Taking that one step further, don't they also have to buy, want or need enough of it to make pursuing them worthwhile? There is almost always a cost attached to acquiring a new customer. It may be small or large, but it should never be ignored.

Beyond all of that, I recommend taking the qualification process one more step. In order to consider someone a *fully qualified prospect*, they have to show some real interest in buying from you. Remember, the buying decision is about products *and* suppliers. The first two qualifying criteria address the products. The third one addresses you as the supplier.

What Is Selling?

It's pretty obvious that *selling* means different things to different people. Some of us think of it as an honorable profession. Others equate salespeople with slithering reptiles. But as I noted earlier, at the most fundamental level, your business is about selling something to somebody, so some level of selling has to happen.

I don't think that has to mean hard-chargin', deal-makin', close-or-die selling, although there probably are situations in which that's appropriate. Selling cars, for example, involves a sense of urgency, because the whole auto industry knows that if they let you off the lot, you might not come back. Think about that, and again, consider *the ability to choose between different products and suppliers.* When I bought my last car, I looked at several different brands, and when I settled on a brand and model, I talked to two different dealers. I bought the car from the second dealer, largely because the deals were almost identical – and I'd basically had enough!

There's something else to consider here, though. Not only were the deals essentially the same, so were the salespeople. Salesperson 1 didn't give me a good enough reason to return to him. Or to put that another way, he didn't fully *engage* with me. I can't honestly say that Salesperson 2 did a much better job, so maybe he benefitted from the luck of the draw, but I hope you'll agree that Salesperson 1 had an opportunity he didn't capitalize on.

That takes us back to the question of what selling is, and here's how I define it. *Selling is the act of helping suspects, prospects and customers to make the decision to buy from you.* I hope that sounds more like *consultative* selling and less like hard-chargin', deal-makin', etc. I hope it also sounds like the kind of selling you personally want to be engaged in.

Now let's consider that selling, consultative or otherwise, often starts before a buyer and salesperson engage. In fact, a large part of the engagement process can occur before the participants reach the Point of Sale.

Advertising

How important is *advertising* to your business? Maybe I should rephrase that and simply state that advertising is *very* important to your business, and you're probably not doing enough of it – and the advertising you are doing is probably not as effective as it could be!

That raises the question of the purpose of advertising. I often ask small business owners and managers what they hope to get out of their advertising, and the most typical answer is something along the lines of "keeping our name in front of our customers." OK, that can be an engagement strategy, but is it all that advertising could be/should be doing for you? And while advertising can definitely keep your name in front of your customers, how about your suspects and prospects? The real issue here is whether a one-size-fits-all advertising strategy is likely to work for you. My position is that you should engage each category differently – suspects, prospects, customers and maximized customers.

At the core of the following diagram is the Point of Sale. This is where your "sales team" comes into direct contact with your customers and potential customers. That term may require some explanation, so let's relate it back to my definition of selling: *Your sales team consists of any/every individual within your company who has opportunity to help a suspect, prospect or customer make the decision to buy from you.* That may be someone whose title has "sales" in it, or someone whose title has "customer" in it, (Customer Service Representative, for example), or someone else for whom engaging with customers and potential customers is either understood to be – or ends up by necessity to be – part of the job description. The "direct contact" can be face-to-face, voice-to-voice, written word (email, text, social media or even an old-fashioned letter), or any combination thereof. The key point is that advertising is "long-distance" engagement, hopefully leading to direct contact at the Point of Sale.

(You'll note, by the way, that I didn't put *maximized customers* in this diagram, although they are hopefully a subset of your current customer base. As noted, we'll get to them later on.)

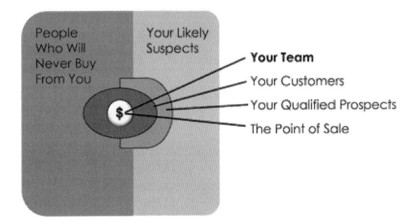

For now, please note the two largest elements, your *likely suspects* and the people who will never buy from you. You will accept, I hope, that some people will fit into that second category. Here's some more fundamental knowledge: *You can't sell to everybody!* I wish you could. I wish *I* could! But that's an unreasonable – and therefore unhealthy – expectation.

The first challenge in selling is to separate those two largest categories. The idea, of course, is to put most of your engagement resources into situations that are most likely to provide a return on your investment.

In the advertising world, the terms "shotgun" and "rifle" are popular. The analogy is pretty basic, "shotgun" implies wide and "rifle" implies narrow in terms of targeting parameters. I'm sure you'll agree that being able to narrow your focus is probably better strategy, but let's start at the point where you really can't, where you have a universe of suspects, but you have no way of knowing which are *likely* suspects, and which are people who will never, ever buy from you.

Selling To People

Before we go further, here's another fundamental concept. People sell to people. Companies also sell to people. But neither people nor companies ever sell successfully to companies. That's pretty straightforward when we're talking about B2C – Business to Consumer. But it needs to be equally clear when we're talking about B2B – Business to Business. I don't care whether you sell products or services or tangibles or intangibles or commodities or custom manufactured widgets, you have to make the sale to a person, or possibly even a group of people. Your suspects, prospects, customers and maximized customers may work for little mom-and-pops, medium-sized non-profits, huge public corporations, or anywhere in between, but those terms still apply to *people*.

I use the term "account" to identify the company in B2B selling. And I want you to consider that you can have multiple customers within an account. You can, in fact, have suspects, prospects, customers and maximized customers within a single account, all at the same time. When we get to Customer Maximization, part of what we'll be talking about is making sure to identify and engage with all of the likely suspects in any company or organization you're working with.

It's also important, though, to understand that the same thing can apply to B2C. For example, I have a family membership at a local fitness club. It's just my wife and I, but that still means two separate *customers* they have to engage with in order to maintain the overall relationship. If they don't meet each of our individual needs and expectations, they may not keep either of us as customers.

Now, back to shotguns and rifles, and an unseparated universe of suspects. Let's make the size of the universe 25,000 – a small city somewhere in America. Let's make the business a fitness club, much like the one I belong to. And let's make it their goal to add 250 new customers, with a series of ads in the local newspaper as the first step in the process.

Suspect Engagement

What should these ads say? First and foremost, an effective advertisement must make it clear exactly what's for sale. This is a specific area where just "keeping your name in front of" anybody can be a recipe for failure. The question right here is whether your name conveys what you sell. The club I belong to is called O2 Fitness. I think that name by itself has a pretty good chance of connecting. I once drove by a place called The Cardio Center. Was it a fitness club, or specialized medical office? *Engagement is all about communication, and real communication requires that both the sender and the receiver connect all the dots.*

In the case of a newspaper ad – or any other form of static advertising, which would include billboards and direct mail and even a banner ad on a website – those dots also have to be connected pretty quickly. How quickly? I found a number of articles online that referenced a 2015 study done by Microsoft in Canada, which indicated that modern humans have an average attention span of only 8 seconds. (Modern goldfish, by comparison, have an average attention span of 9 seconds, but I think it's fair to say that they lead less complicated lives!)

The point I'm hoping to make here is that engagement is a process, which means that it's usually best accomplished in steps or stages. The first stage of suspect engagement with static advertising is to capture attention. The second stage is to establish interest. The third stage, if interest is indeed present, is to motivate action – in other words, to create movement toward The Point Of Sale. Here's an observation, though: Most static advertising fails at the first stage.

How do you avoid that? The best way to capture attention is the effective use of words and images. By words, in this context, I specifically mean a headline. By images, I mean graphics that can stand on their own as well as supporting the headline. Here's a headline/graphics combination for a bad ad:

The Cardio Center
(An image of the building exterior)

Here's what I think would be a better combination:

Do you want to get fitter?
Get stronger? Get healthier?
(An image of a fit, strong, healthy
looking person working out.)

Here's another observation. Most small business owners and managers are not great marketers, either strategically or creatively. That's nothing to be ashamed of, but it is something to be aware of. And it may put you in a position where you need better strategy and/or more creativity than you're capable of on your own. OK, if you're not a competent plumber, you would engage with someone else to do that kind of work for you, right? You have the same opportunity with copywriting, graphic design, and overall advertising/marketing strategy. If you don't have a necessary skill or experience, engage with someone who does!

Signage's Role

As I just mentioned, I once drove by a place called The Cardio Center. I never actually saw the business itself, which was located in a strip mall. What I saw was the business's name on a pylon sign along the roadway.

Please consider that this sort of signage is another form of "static advertising." In fact, it has a dual role in the advertising/engagement process. It's primary role is probably to say "Here We Are!" – possibly after other advertising motivated the action to actually visit the Point of Sale. But signage also has potential to capture *initial attention* on its own. How many times have you driven by a place and flashed on the signage, thinking: "Hey, I'm interested in that!"

Beyond that, how many times have you *walked* past a store and flashed on its window or wall graphics?

Trade Show Signage

Here's a similar application. Have you ever attended or exhibited at a trade show? The typical attendee walks the aisles, looking quickly at each booth or exhibit, with one primary question in mind: *"Am I interested in what they sell?"* I think it's fair to say that most trade show attendees qualify as *likely suspects* – some level of interest brought them to the site of the show. Your goal as an exhibitor is to engage them in the short time it takes them to pass by your booth or table. How do you do that? *The best way to capture attention is the effective use of words and images.*

The worst way, as an aside, is to stand in the aisle, grabbing attendees and pulling them into your area. Don't laugh, I've had that happen to me!

What's For Sale?

Going back to our suspect engagement scenario, on a basic level, what's for sale in these ads is a membership in a fitness club. On a deeper level, though, it's the benefit(s) to be gained through membership in a fitness club. Do you see how that's reflected in my suggested headline? And don't forget, on a still deeper level, it's the benefit(s) to be gained through membership in *this* fitness club.

This is a good place to talk about the FAB Formula – Features, Advantages and Benefits. Let's give our fictional fitness club some attractive features. It has a wide range of strength-building and cardiovascular equipment. It has a pool, a steam-room, a sauna and plush locker rooms. It has free, 24/7 child care. It has a Healthy Eats Café that serves breakfast, lunch and dinner. It's conveniently located with plenty of parking.

Sounds great, right? But you need to understand that no one will join this club just because of those features. They will only join if the features are *meaningful to them* and provide a *real benefit*. For example, I'm an empty nester. I don't care about free, 24/7 child care. In fact, it's possible that this feature would provide a disincentive for me, because the child care isn't really free. It would be more correct to say that it carries no *additional* charge. But every member's dues includes a percentage that pays for that child care, so I'm paying for it whether I use it or not.

On the other hand, I like steam and sauna and especially plush locker rooms. The last club we belonged to was, to put it kindly, highly functional. It had a wide range of equipment – certainly everything I needed in that regard – but the physical space was pretty spartan and the locker room left a lot to be desired. So when we read about O2 Fitness, the fact that they offered these *features* gave them a competitive *advantage* over our previous club, because they provided us with a meaningful *benefit* that the other club couldn't match.

Second Stage

The second stage of suspect engagement with static advertising is to establish interest.

The title notwithstanding, it was never our intention to write this book as a list of rules. If we had, though, this would be Rule 1: *Engagement is an interrogatory process, not a declaratory process.* In other words, you engage by asking, not telling. Sure, the *telling* is a part of the overall process, but it's not the most important part. Look back at the headline on our ad example. Questions, right? *Do you want to get fitter? Get stronger? Get healthier?*

Remember that part of the goal here is to separate the likely suspects from the people who will never buy from you. What we're hoping for is a simple yes-or-no answer, because it's fair to expect that anyone who says *yes* will read on. Obviously, anyone who says *no* probably won't, but that's OK, they've separated themselves. To put it differently, they've *disqualified* themselves.

Now, what about someone who says *maybe* when they see your ad? This is where *repetition* enters our discussion. There have been numerous studies on the effect of repetition in advertising, and it's been pretty well proven that readership and response follow a bell curve. Independent of the effect of *better* words and/or images, more people will give attention to your ad the second time they see it, and probably still more the third time. The "more" effect will continue until your ad reaches the saturation point, which means that most of the likely suspects will have already seen and responded to it, and most of the unlikely's will have already seen and rejected it.

As for the maybe's: *Oh, this again. Yes, I'm interested, I need to take the next step this time.* Or: *No, I'm not really interested. I thought I might be, but I'm not.*

I can't tell you the "right" number of placements, by the way. I can only tell you to track the performance of any advertising campaign. When activity slows down, you've probably reached or passed the saturation point. When activity stops altogether, you should probably stop running that ad!

Back to the ad itself, the headline and graphics either will or will not capture attention. If they do, they either will or will not establish *immediate* interest, all by themselves. Happily, you don't have to depend on that – unless your ad is so small that a headline and limited graphics are all you have room for. That raises the question of how large your ad should be, which connects to the question of how much you can afford to invest in your ad/engagement campaign.

Investment Attitude

Invest is a key word. Advertising is all about spending money to make more money. The cost of advertising is only one half of the equation, though, and if you'll forgive me some questionable math, it needs to be the smaller half. You have to have an *investment attitude* in order to be a successful marketer.

OK, then, how much should our fictional fitness club be willing to invest in its ad campaign? Let's go back to the goal of adding 250 new members. Now let's estimate the revenue result of reaching that goal. If the average membership produces $600 in annual revenue, then the ROI – Return On Investment – calculation could be based on $150,000 in increased revenue over the next 12 months.

There's a flaw in that math, though. Do you see it?

In order to end up with the full $150,000, all of the new members have to join up pretty much immediately, and that's unlikely to happen. Remember the bell curve! If I were doing the ROI forecast for this campaign, I might base it on gaining 10 new members the first month, 20 the second month, 40 the third month, 60 each in months four and five, 30 in month six, 20 in month seven and 10 in month eight. Each individual membership is still worth $600 over *its* first 12 months, but the campaign would now generate "only" $107,000 over the next 12 months. ("Only" because $107,000 is less than $150,000. I'm pretty sure that gaining 250 new members over any timeframe is still well worth doing.)

Now our investment equation has its anchor point. The question becomes, how much should our fictional fitness club be willing to invest in order to gain a return of $107,000 in revenue? Here's my answer: *I don't know!*

The reason I'm saying that is that *investment tolerance* is an individual decision. I know people who would happily invest fifty cents to return a dollar. I know others who require a 10X or greater return. Some of that is the cost of *servicing* each new customer, which would probably be relatively small for a fitness club, but much larger for, say, a lawn care contractor. Even assuming that all of the equipment was paid for, the $35 I used to pay my lawn guy every 2 weeks during mowing season had to pay wages for the 2-man crew that showed up to do the work, plus fuel for the truck, the mower and the two gas trimmers. It certainly wasn't $35 in profit! My fitness club, on the other hand, could probably accommodate 250 more members with little, if any, incremental cost attached.

Spending Decisions

For the sake of discussion, let's put our fitness club's tolerance at 5X. That means a projected return of $107,000 justifies an advertising investment of $21,400. Again for the sake of discussion, let's say that a quarter-page ad in the newspaper costs $800 per insertion and an eighth-page ad costs $450. At those rates, a budget of $21,400 would support 26 quarter-page placements plus some change, or 47 eighth-page placements plus some change.

There might be a flaw in *that* math, though. What if our fitness club needs help on the creative end? Let's say it does, so we have to pay for that. If we budget $1400 for creative, we're now left with enough money for 25 quarter-page placements or 44 eighth-page placements (plus some change.)

So now the question is, which size ad is the better size to accomplish the goal. On one hand, bigger is generally better in terms of both capturing attention and generating interest. On the other hand, more repetition is generally better than less. The core issue, though, is how much space is *necessary* to tell a story that will engage likely suspects.

I would approach this by turning my designer loose to show me options – two or perhaps three options for each size, and maybe even two or three options for an even smaller ad. By options, I mean different "looks" and/or different combinations of words and images. The options would lead to discussions, and eventually to a final decision. Please note that I'm ultimately letting the ad tell me how big it needs to be!

Please also note that this in an engagement exercise on two separate levels. I'm engaging with my designer in order to develop an ad that will (hopefully) engage my suspect universe. That designer might be an internal resource, in which case it's employee engagement. He or she might be an outside resource, in which case it's supplier engagement. Either way, I'm talking about a process of ideas/options leading to discussion, leading to refinement, leading to more discussion, and eventually resulting in a strategy. I'm talking about two heads being better than one. In fact, I would probably involve even more heads, hopefully stopping just short of having too many cooks in this particular kitchen.

I recently completed an exercise like this with one of my clients. She gave her designer three elements of guidance: a list of features she wanted to stress, a group of images she thought would be appropriate, and a final instruction: to make the ad as big as it had to be but also as small as it could be and still get the job done.

When the designer, in this case a graphic artist employed by a local printing company, came back with initial options, the two of them sat down for an "I like this a lot, I like this a little, I don't like this at all" conversation. Then my client said, "Before you go back to your drawing board, let me show these to a couple of my people to see what they think."

My client later told me that those employee conversations were the most important part of the process. "They liked most of what I liked, but they also liked some of what I didn't like, and they brought up a couple of really good ideas that I think made the whole thing considerably better. And two of the three of them also thanked me for letting them participate."

To put that differently, two of her three employees thanked her for *engaging* them in the process.

****

We have a lot more to talk about in terms of advertising and engaging with suspects, prospects, customers and maximized customers. But I've raised an example of engaging with employees, and I think that makes it a good time to hear from Brian on that subject.

2 Employee Engagement
Brian Adam

I am a people person. Dave had that exactly right. It has been said that a stranger is just a friend you haven't met yet, and that's been my mantra throughout my life. I love people. I love being around people. I draw energy from them. I'm a true extrovert. And even beyond that, I seem to have a severe case of FOMO – Fear Of Missing Out! – so from a party to a networking event to a business opportunity, I want to be there and I want to be involved.

As Dave wrote earlier, we met at a conference in Las Vegas, where we both spoke to a group of small business owners on "Essential Small Business Strategies." I was impressed by his content, but also by his speaking style. He really engaged the audience. I have a lot less speaking experience, so I was taking copious notes on both his content and his delivery.

In his presentation that day, and in his introduction to this book, Dave referenced his first sales job in 1978. I was born in 1978! So I don't have his 40+ years of business experience and I don't have the same presentation skills. I also don't have an MBA and quite honestly, I'm not that smart. I am certainly not a Mensa-genius! But I have had some success in business.

Why? I think it's simply that I used my strengths to compensate for my shortcomings, and my greatest strength is my love of people. If I could harness my interpersonal skills, I thought, I could use my "extrovert-ness" to create a great corporate culture. I'd recruit some great people – people better and smarter and greater than me. I'd get them engaged and excited about working with me. With them, I'd build a successful company. I'd make this business thing work out, for them and for me.

In theory and in practice, that's been working pretty well. I'm excited about providing you with more detail on what we've done – what's worked, what's failed and some *engagement* tips and best practices I've learned along the way. Before that, though, I'd like to give you some context and share my story with you.

My Family

In 1950, my father was born on a farm in a tiny town called Kleekamp, in East Germany. He lived the first couple of years of his life under Communism. When he was a young boy, his father, mother and he and his two brothers packed up, left their extended family and all of their possessions and risked their lives attempting to escape through the Berlin Wall. They could not say good bye to friends or family. They could not bring any possessions with them. They were lucky. My family made it through the wall with the help of many others in East Germany who risked their own lives to help families like mine escape. They were airlifted from West Berlin to West Germany, where they spent two years in a refugee camp outside of Hamburg. Eventually they were sponsored and immigrated to the United States with nothing more than the clothes on their backs – and the debt from the boat ride!

They settled in Milwaukee, Wisconsin where some cousins had settled a couple of years earlier. My grandparents, who had once enjoyed a fairly comfortable life on a farm, now worked a 2nd shift job in a steel mill and a part-time job cleaning houses. They never looked back, though. They worked hard, raised their 3 boys and glowed as the family grew to include grandchildren, and then numerous great-grandchildren. We lost my grandfather four years ago, and my grandmother last year. Both lived into their 90's. I'm not sure I'll ever be able to fully appreciate the sacrifices they made, and the risks that they and my father and my uncles took to ensure that my generation had the opportunity to live a better life.

Entrepreneurial Spirit

Why did they leave? What was their motivation? Obviously, part of it was escaping Communism. But deep down, I also believe that my family had the entrepreneurial spirit. They wanted to control their own destiny. They wanted a better life. They wanted the opportunity to work hard, to be successful, to fail if it came to that, but to do it on their terms.

All of this helped shape my journey and who I am today. A big part of my motivation is to provide a great life for my own family. All of this also provides great perspective on life. Rough day? Lost a big sale? Yeah, that doesn't seem so devastating when I reflect back on my grandparents. No matter how hard, challenging or frustrating life or business can be, I will never face the same challenges that my grandparents faced, or the same challenges that millions of people around the world today face.

Olympus Group

Now on to Olympus. My father, Helmut, acquired Olympus Group in 1992. After years of working for a publicly traded company, he'd had enough, and wanted to call his own shots. He spent over a year researching possibilities and really sort of stumbled on this 75-person print, cut & sew shop. At that time Olympus was a printer and sewer of flags, banners and mascot costumes. Yes, mascot costumes! Olympus made Ronald McDonald's outfit, the first Grimace and Birdie, and helped create the Milwaukee Brewers Racing Sausages and countless other characters for professional sports franchises, brand icons and universities.

While the mascot business was undeniably cool, most of the revenue came from flags. Olympus manufactured and sold U.S. flags, state flags and a variety of stock flags to retailers, primarily large mass merchants like Menards & Home Depot. It was a good, steady business. Then in early 1991, the first Gulf War began, Operation Desert Storm, with Norman Schwarzkopf and Colin Powell.

Historically, whenever there is a war or crisis, patriotism and U.S. flag sales soar – sometimes by a factor of 5X or even 10X. Almost overnight, Olympus had orders for LOTS & LOTS of U.S. flags. The previous owners purchased raw materials and began production. Everyone was excited, they were going to crank out U.S. flags, so proud citizens could display those flags outside their homes and offices. It was projected to be a record year for Olympus. But something happened. The war ended – quickly.

Retailers, who had placed large orders, immediately canceled them, Instead of having a record year, Olympus was stuck with several "normal" years' worth of raw materials and saddled with the associated debt. The materials weren't going to go bad, of course, but instead of selling the flags in 3-4 months, it was likely to take 3-4 years. It was a catastrophe for Olympus.

The company wasn't going to be able to service the debt and bankruptcy seemed inevitable.

For my father, though, this was an opportunity, a chance to live the Entrepreneurial American Dream. He was able to acquire Olympus for very little cash, but he obviously had a major issue on his hands. How do you survive with notes and payables that are due today, but materials you're not going to be able to sell for the next 3-4 years? He went right to work on the problem, engaged with the creditors, negotiated for more flexible terms and invested the next eight years of his life in Olympus' resurrection. And he successfully turned the business around, and built a profitable company that he and his family could be proud of.

Though it's not the main part of the business anymore, Olympus still produces U.S. flags, and continues to make some of the quirkiest and most recognizable mascots around.

Personal History

I grew up in the business. I packed boxes in the shipping department, ran grommet machines, pulled screen-printing squeegees, slid poles into pole pockets, cut the grass outside and I was even occasionally allowed to help make the mascots. (I personally installed fans inside of "Magic Sprinkles" head – a short-lived mascot for the Ponderosa Steakhouse chain). My role in those years required no artistic ability and very little skill, which was fortunate, because I certainly did not possess either. But it was a great "family" job in a great family business.

After high school, I went off to college at the University of Wisconsin-Madison – with no intention of ever coming back to the family business! Olympus was a great company, and I was proud of my family business, but print was not the sexiest industry in the world, and it was not something that really excited me. In other words, I just wasn't *engaged*.

While in Madison, I got a degree in marketing and accounting. I had interest in sales and marketing and I was definitely *engaged* in those classes. While I was less passionate about the crunching of numbers, I ultimately decided that an accounting degree would provide me with a valuable perspective on whatever business I found myself in, and would complement the "soft" skills I learned in my marketing classes.

Now on to the most memorable part of my college education. I used my mascot background/experience and successfully auditioned to be Bucky Badger, the UW mascot. The extrovert inside me loved every minute! I performed at countless sporting events in front of thousands of fans. I got to make people laugh – even better, to make kids smile! – and I was able to hone what I considered to be some pretty above-average dance moves.

I even received some national notoriety. In 1999, during a Wisconsin vs. Michigan State football game at Camp Randall in Madison, I "borrowed" a Michigan State cheerleader flag (coincidentally, a product manufactured by Olympus), and took the flag down to the east end zone right by our student section. I threw the flag to the ground and stomped on it (sorry Michigan State fans!) One of their cheerleaders took exception to this, ran down the sideline, sized me up, and completely laid me out with a perfect, textbook tackle. I never saw him coming. Boom! It may have been the hardest hit of the day. In fact, the headlines and clips were all over USA Today, Fox Sports, and ESPN. "Bucky Badger gets Owned" "Cheerleader Flattens Bucky" "Michigan State's Defense Couldn't Tackle But Their Cheerleaders Can." You can still watch the clip on YouTube. If you're in need of a quick laugh, search "Michigan State Cheerleader + Bucky Badger."

Well, That's Interesting!

So now you might be thinking, "OK Brian, that's an interesting story (at least the part about you getting beat up by a cheerleader) but why should we listen to you? What credibility do you have?" Obviously, I did go back to the family business, so let me share with you a few of the things that we've accomplished, since I took over from my father and became President in 2006:

- Olympus has grown from $10 million in revenue and 75 employees to more than $30 million in revenue and 200 employees
- We went from one facility (Milwaukee) to four (Milwaukee, Orlando, Denver & Grand Rapids)
- More than 10% of our team members are "boomerang employees" – meaning they worked at Olympus, took an opportunity somewhere else, and then came back to Olympus.

- In 2017, Glassdoor named me one of its Top 25 CEOs To Work For (based on anonymous feedback from employees. I was 25th on the list so I guess I was really lucky they didn't do a Top 24 list!)

Now let me tell you what I'm *most* proud of. What we have done is to build a great little company, that values its employees, rewards them for their contributions, and because of this, has outperformed others in our industry over the last 10 years.

Please note that I said *we*. *We* have some great people who care about what *we* do, are invested in *our* success and are outperforming *our* competitors. We're far from perfect, but I think you'll agree that neither are Apple or Google or any of the other "big guys." Our goal is to be a little better today than we were yesterday and then be a little better tomorrow than we are today. Our core strategy is to be fully engaged as a team.

I think the true measure of engagement is that team. And the kind of engagement we strive for doesn't – and didn't – happen overnight. It's not a management fad. Getting employees engaged takes time and it's a never-ending process. So moving forward, I'm going to share some of the things that have worked at Olympus. My hope is that you can take a couple of these "tips and tricks" and apply them where you work, in turn creating a better, more *engaging* place to for you and your teammates to work.

Why It Matters

Why does "fully engaged as a team" matter? I think most employers feel like they treat their employees well. *"We pay them well and provide them with benefits."* Most companies believe they have a good corporate culture and that their team members are aligned around common goals. They further believe that their team members, for the most part, like their jobs and have no intention of leaving.

They're probably wrong! According to a recent study by Gallup, only one-third of all employees are really engaged. Think about that. This data suggests that only one out of every three employees truly cares about where they work, are passionate about what they do, are loyal to who they work with and work for. Two out of every three employees are at least thinking about working somewhere else, if not actively looking for another job.

Certainly there's a margin for error in this data, but just as certainly, there's more *disengagement* out there than most small business owners and managers think. And because of that, most small businesses underperform.

On the other side of the coin, the benefits of real engagement are significant. According to a study by the Hay Group, engaged employees are:

- 31% more productive
- 70% stronger on customer service
- Generate 37% higher sales
- Display 3x more creativity
- Are 5x more likely to recommend their company

This study's bottom line suggests that companies with engaged employees outperform those without engaged employees by 202%

Let's go back to the "negative" side of the coin. An even more recent (2019) study by ADP Research Institute produced the following data:

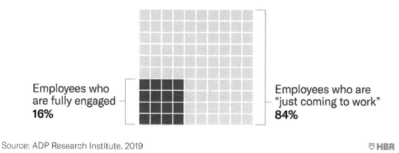

The Sad State of Employee Engagement

The vast majority of employees globally aren't fully engaged with their work.

Employees who are fully engaged **16%**

Employees who are "just coming to work" **84%**

Source: ADP Research Institute, 2019 ⓊHBR

If that doesn't scare you, I don't know why! We all spend a lot of time at our jobs. Think about this statistic: The average American will spend 36% of his or her adult life at work. We'll spend more time at work than anywhere else except possibly our beds – and, by the way, do any of us entrepreneurs really get enough sleep? If we're going to spend that much time at one place, isn't it paramount that we enjoy and are passionate about what we do? And not just *"we"* referring to business owners and managers. "We" as in everybody!

So how do we create *engaged* employees? How do we get employees to enjoy what they do, and truly care about the place where they work? Read on, we're getting to the good stuff.

3 Purpose, Values and Voice
Brian Adam

Are your employees working for a paycheck, punching the clock, counting down the minutes until they can go home? Or are they working for a purpose, working at something they truly believe in, and where they care about and are invested in the outcome? Are they energized by what they are doing, and is that having an impact on their – and your – results?

If you want engaged employees, they need to have a purpose – and for the record "to make the owner or external shareholders rich" is not a very motivating purpose! Think about some of the most successful (and profitable) companies in the world. Their missions don't speak to *return on capital* or *maximizing shareholder value*. They all stand for something greater.

- Walmart - *We save people money so they live better.*
- Google – *To organize the world's information and make it universally accessible and useful.*
- Amazon – *To be the Earth's most customer-centric company, where customers can find anything they might want to buy online.*
- Southwest –*Dedication to the highest quality of Customer Service delivered with a sense of warmth, friendliness, individual pride and Company Spirit.*

Four of the most successful companies in the United States have mission statements that have nothing to do with shareholder value or profit. There's a "more" to their missions, a greater good. This deeper meaning is something employees can wake up to and get excited about being a part of. Creating purpose is an absolutely critical step in employee engagement.

Believe And Support

I know what you might be thinking: "That's great Brian, but I'm not Walmart, Google, Amazon or Southwest. How can my business create something that motivating?" Or maybe you're thinking: "Will my employees really support a cause? Won't they see through it? Our goal really *is* to make money. Isn't that every businesses' fundamental goal?"

Yes, a "for profit" business is intended to make and maximize profit. But that and the "more" factor are not mutually exclusive. Maximizing profit and creating a greater good can co-exist. In fact the more money a company makes, the more it can help them to advance their mission.

TOMS (the shoe company) is a great example. Here's how they express their mission: *With every product purchased, TOMS will help a person in need, One for One®.* It all started with shoes, and to date, TOMS has helped give over 70 million new pairs of shoes in over 70 countries around the world. If you bought a pair, they gave a pair, so the more they sold, the more they gave. Their mission has expanded to restoring sight, providing safe water, supporting safe birth, and ending bullying.

At Olympus, we are not as grandiose in our purpose as TOMS, but I do believe we've created a motivating mission for our team. Hopefully our journey can help and inspire you to clarify your own purpose.

Then and Now

When I joined Olympus this was our mission statement: *Olympus Flag & Banner, Inc. prints, sews, designs and assembles quality products (which include flags, banners and promotional costumes/mascots), adapting its manufacturing process to meet the changing needs of a broad customer base while offering the Olympus team a respectful environment in which the individual may grow and prosper with the company.*

While this accurately describes what we did and what we stood for, I'd argue that it's less than an inspiring mission. I don't think anyone joined Olympus because of what we stood for, nor was anyone popping out of bed in the morning, feeling inspired to help us "print, sew, design and assemble a quality product."

As we thought about our future, and where the company was headed, we wanted to simplify our mission. The goal was to ensure that it inspired our team members, and that it withstood the test of time. Personally, I'm not smart enough to invent anything new, so as you saw earlier, we took a look at some of the better known and most successful organizations in the world and reviewed their missions. Here are a few more of the good ones:

- American Cancer Society: *Our mission is to save lives, celebrate lives, and lead the fight for a world without cancer.*
- Tesla: *Our mission is to accelerate the world's transition to sustainable energy. Tesla was founded in 2003 by a group of engineers who wanted to prove that people didn't need to compromise to drive electric – that electric vehicles can be better, quicker and more fun to drive than gasoline cars.*
- Mayo Clinic: *To inspire hope, and contribute to health and well-being by providing the best care to every patient through integrated clinical practice, education and research. Mayo Clinic will provide an unparalleled experience as the most trusted partner for health care.*
- One Drop: *We aim to ensure sustainable access to safe water and sanitation for the most vulnerable communities through innovative partnerships, creativity and the power of art.*
- Glaxo Smith Kline: *Our mission is to help people do more, feel better, live longer.*

OK, at Olympus, we're not fighting cancer, designing energy-efficient vehicles or trying to bring clean water to the entire world. We print and sew, and we recognize there's not a lot that's inspiring about that. But our philosophy has always been to treat our employees well, to take care of our team members in the expectation that they'll take care of our customers and bend over backwards to help them. So, could that be our inspiring mission? After much deliberation, we developed this new mission statement:

At Olympus, we want to create
a rewarding work environment for our team.

Short and Simple

That's it. It's short, it's simple, and we've found that it means different things to different people. I have to tell you that our business advisors weren't big fans. They felt we needed to include something about return on investment. *"Brian, you're not a non-profit. Your mission has to include a return on capital."*

I wholeheartedly agree that generating a return is important and would actually help us achieve the mission. The more money we make, the easier it is to create a rewarding work environment, right? But I also felt strongly that this was a mission *for our team.* I am personally motivated to be profitable. They don't need to be! They do need a *purpose* that resonates with their own self-interest. I see it as a simple progression: *If we create a rewarding work environment for our team, we'll have* engaged *team members, and they will outperform our competitors, and that will provide the return we're looking for.*

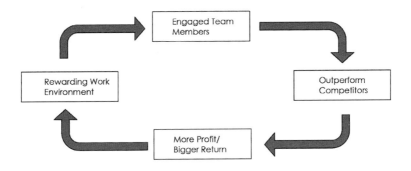

We also took some time to articulate what a "rewarding work environment" meant to us. Again, we tried to keep it fairly simple. At Olympus, we define a rewarding work environment as a place where:

1. You take pride in what you do.
2. You are compensated fairly.
3. You can work in a safe and comfortable environment.
4. You are empowered to learn and grow.

Let's break those down:

You take pride in what you do – At the end of the day, if you walk away from your job with a sense of pride in what you accomplished, you feel good, and you most likely feel *engaged*. Think about the jobs you've loved. I would bet that, in every one of those roles, you felt an innate sense of pride in what you did, what you accomplished and what you contributed.

You are compensated fairly – None of us works for free. (Well, maybe a very small percentage of us don't care at all about the money. All of the rest of us expect to get paid for our work!) To support the employee engagement we're all looking for, we need to pay our team members a competitive wage *and* offer meaningful benefits. I'm not suggesting that you *overpay* what an employee is worth to your company. That ultimately puts you at a competitive disadvantage. But underpaying – especially with your star performers – too often leads to *disengagement* and attrition. And please make note of this, paying a *competitive* wage is the absolute floor for every employee. What they're worth to your company might be well above that floor. Again, not *overpaying*, but understanding and reflecting true worth.

You can work in a safe and comfortable environment – *Safe* and *comfortable* probably have different meanings to different types of businesses. In an office environment, for example, *safe* may be mostly about security. In a manufacturing company like Olympus, we have that, but we also have lasers and blades and fork lifts and other machines with all sorts of moving parts. You can get HURT on our shop floor if you and your teammates are not fully attuned to *safety first*. Getting hurt is a big deal, so we make a big deal out of safety.

We take *comfortable* seriously too, in ways that many manufacturing companies apparently don't. For example, we have air conditioning in all our facilities, not just the office space, but also the shop floor. We're not a spa by any means, but we believed from the start that a well-lit, temperature controlled, safe environment would support employee engagement, and all the evidence says that it has. I mentioned earlier than we have a lot of "boomerang" employees, and this is one of the things they tend to mention when they come back to work for us.

Here's one of my favorite employee engagement stories. We recently renovated our restrooms – at considerable cost, I might add. A month or so afterward, I overheard a tenured employee talking to a new hire and explaining: "Man, you just don't get it. Olympus *cares* about you. They even care about where you (here he used a word I won't subject you to, a euphemism for going to the bathroom). This place is great!"

You are empowered to learn and grow – I believe most people have an innate desire to learn and grow. By giving our team members the ability to learn more – to grow into new roles, to move up and advance their careers – it increases their level of engagement. I can't remember ever hearing anyone say: "You know what, I hope I just do the same job at the same level for the next 20 years." (Let me qualify that. I don't think I ever heard *anyone of the caliber I really want on our team* say anything like that.)

We try to promote from within whenever possible, and I'm proud to say that more than 70% of our current managers and supervisors were internal promotions. In addition to the way they do their jobs, this fact alone makes them role models for everyone below the supervisory level. In our culture, *moving up* is more than just a possibility. Our team members see evidence of that every day.

From a management perspective, if we can achieve those four objectives, we've done our job. More importantly, when our employees feel that we've accomplished these 4 things, we see and feel their engagement and we see the results.

Four Tips for Creating Your Mission Statement

1. Ask your employees: "Other than a paycheck, why do you work here?" Get their feedback on what makes your company special.
2. Make "the test of time" an integral part of the process. This is not something you want to have to revisit and change with any sort of frequency.
3. Ensure it's meaningful to your employees – your mission statement is NOT for your customers, suppliers, bankers or lawyers. This is for your team. It's *their* purpose! Make sure it's designed with them in mind.
4. Do some homework – research what others have written.

Core Values

The next step in our process was to define our core values. These are the traits you look for in your employees to help you achieve your mission. You consider these traits when making hiring decisions, promotion decisions and calculating annual pay increases. You also consider them when you're faced with less pleasant decisions about what to do with poor performers.

Core values should remain consistent and embody the ethos of your organization. Core values should rarely, if ever, change. In full disclosure, we did change one of our core values but I'll get into that later.

How did we create our core values? When I purchased Olympus, we did not have any. To define our core values, we polled all of our managers and asked them to identify the 3-5 employees whom they felt best embodied Olympus. Who would we place on a pedestal to show the world what makes us great? Who are your superstars on your teams. Then we got together in one room and put the names on a whiteboard, and not surprisingly, a core group of employees appeared multiple times across numerous managers' lists.

Next, we asked our managers to identify the traits that earned each employee a place on the list. *Why did you put this guy, or this woman, on your list? What specifically do you like/appreciate/respect about this individual?*

After some lively discussion, we decided that four specific traits defined our superstars:

1. Selflessness
2. "Can Do" Attitudes
3. Creativity & Innovation
4. Integrity

We then started talking with our team members about these core values, and integrating them into our personnel decisions. But over the course of the next 12 months, we realized that something didn't feel right. We're an innovative company, we make mascots, we have graphic designers on staff and do all sorts of uber-creative things. But some of our superstar employees didn't really exhibit "creativity & innovation." Kwai, one of our seamstresses, was a perfect example. She had a great attitude, was a team player, a very high character individual, and she sewed fast – really, really, really fast! – but I can't say that she was especially creative or innovative. There were other examples, like Jon who works in our warehouse. Great attitude, flexible, responsive, and also fast, but he didn't necessarily exhibit innovation in his role, nor did we really expect him to.

If you're doing this right, your best employees should embody all of your core values, and for us, this wasn't the case. But the problem was not with the employees. It was with our definitions. So we decided to drop "Creativity & Innovation" as a core value. Yes, these traits are absolutely critical in certain roles, like on our mascot team, engineering team, or for our technical graphics director, but the need is not universal. As we thought specifically about Kwai, Jon and some of our other superstars we realized what we'd missed the first time around. These people get results. They flat out get the job done, quickly and accurately. It was a "Eureka" moment, and we happily replaced "Creativity & Innovation" with "Gets Results" to round out our core values.

Olympus Group's "Revised" Core Values
  1. Selflessness
    • You put the good of others above the good of yourself
    • You are egoless when searching for the best solutions
  2. "Can Do" Attitudes
    • You do whatever it takes to get the job done
    • You do what's best, not what's easiest
    • You work to find a solution, especially when others think it impossible
  3. Gets Results
    • You consistently deliver amazing results
    • You work fast by working smart
    • You focus relentlessly on a successful outcome
  4. Integrity
    • You do the right thing, even when no one is looking
    • You do what you say and say what you do
    • You take responsibility for your actions

Four Tips for Defining Your Core Values

1. Engage with your Management Team – your managers, supervisors and/or leads: "Which employees best embody our company? If you had to put a few of them on a pedestal to show the world what makes us special, who would they be?"

2. Compare the lists, looking especially for employees who appear on multiple lists

3. Identify the specific traits that make these employees superstars. "Why exactly did you put them on your list?"

4. Take time to accurately identify your core values, including meaningful descriptions. Remember that you must also communicate all of this to everyone on your team, current and future.

I'm sure you'll see the benefit of engaging your managers. I hope you'll also see the benefit of relating this process to your actual superstar employees. You may still end up feeling like there are desirable – maybe even critical – traits lacking in your current top performers, but they still are the best place to start. That way, you'll be "building up" from actual experience as opposed to asking everyone to embrace a "top-down" directive from Senior Management. That's a much better recipe for buy-in (another term for *engagement*) from the whole team!

Five Tips for Living Your Core Values

As noted, you must communicate all of this to everyone on your team, current and future. Let's take that a step farther. You must live your Core Values! They are meaningless unless your team knows them, believes in them and lives by them.

1. Make sure everyone knows your Core Values.

2. Make sure that your Core Values are part of your performance review process

3. Banners, banners, banners! Print lots of banners with your Core Values and put them up everywhere. Sure, it's a shameless plug for banners by the owner of a banner company, but I'm only half-joking here – you do want your Core Values to be front of mind! You want

managers, supervisors, and employees to reference them daily. While I'm not a huge fan of t-shirts, mugs or other tchotchkes as a means for promoting Core Values, I've found every little bit helps. You can't just print a t-shirt and expect your team to live a Core Value, but keeping them front of mind is important!

4. Leaders must embrace Core Values. If your managers and other leaders don't embody your Core Values they are meaningless.

5. Train on Core Values. Take the time to educate your employees and all new hires on your Core Values – articulate what they are, explain why they are important, and share examples of team members have lived your Core Values. This is a huge story-telling opportunity, and many experts will tell you that story-telling is a highly effective way to train. Treat Core Values training just like training for any other required job skill, for every employee in your company.

Giving Team Members a Voice

Baseline (the online business magazine) published a shocking statistic regarding a 2010 survey of thousands of employees: "59% of workers say they often see problems at their companies that management is not aware of." You know what that means, right? Your employees are probably seeing issues that you aren't seeing. They're aware of issues with customers that haven't made it to your level. They know about fellow employees at risk, for any number of reasons. They hear all kinds of rumors circulating, but they aren't speaking up and sharing any of this with you. If this is happening at your company – and it probably is! – you have a fundamental problem *beyond* the day-to-day problems you're not aware of! And it's not an employee problem, it's a management problem – it's an *engagement* problem!

Awareness is the critical first step to your ability to address and correct any problem. It's essential to engage your team members in this problem-finding/problem-solving process.

At Olympus, we thought we were pretty open. We promoted an "open door" policy, and our managers diligently practiced MBWA (Management By Wandering Around – more on that to follow). We encouraged our employees to speak up, and we even had a cute suggestion box in our lunchroom. We were paying at least lip service to soliciting feedback, but I don't think we truly embraced it. The icing on the cake for me was when an employee asked me this question:

"Hey Brian, how many suggestions did you get in the employee suggestion box so far this year?

The answer was both eye-opening and embarrassing: *"One."*

One suggestion! At this point we had 125 employees and that one suggestion was to buy two-ply toilet paper for our company restrooms. We happily obliged, and still have two-ply today, but I'd argue that our program to that point was a failure. We weren't really engaging with our employees. We didn't open an effective channel of communication to solicit their feedback, so we didn't hear what they truly had to say.

Over the years, we have made soliciting – and acting on! – employee feedback a focus. From the day they're hired, our team members are encouraged to complain. Not laterally, of course, but vertically. Complaining *about* us, we tell them, won't help any of us. If you see issues, we want you to complain *to* us. And over the years, I think it's fair to say that we've shown through our actions that we've listened.

To date, we've received more than 2,000 suggestions. We have addressed and taken action on something like 1,500 of them. The other 500 are in a list that we are still working on – and adding to.

Multiple Channels

I think part of the success of this program is that we introduced multiple channels for soliciting and sharing feedback. The first element was a revamp of our suggestion box program, which now includes a caricature of my

admittedly square head. It's no longer just a "suggestion" box, it's a *"Hey Brian!"* box – *"Hey Brian, I've got something I want to tell you!"*

In introducing this program, we made it clear that we're looking for feedback on a wide range of issues: how to improve quality, how to reduce lead-times, how to reduce cost and waste, how to improve employee morale.

And then we put our money where our mouth was and added cash rewards to the program.

Every other week, I select one suggestion at random and pay the person who contributed it $40 cash. It doesn't have to be anything earthshakingly important or a revolutionary idea. The real goal is to get people to speak up and share their opinions on just about any part of the business. I actually want to hear wacky, zany ideas. I want to hear feedback on toilet paper. I want to hear suggestions about improvements to the facility. I want to hear what our team members like and dislike about their jobs.

Here are some of the suggestions I have received over the last 5 years:

- Buy real estate on the moon
- Purchase massage chairs for every employee
- Build a green roof and get some live goats to live on it
- Flood our front yard and freeze it in winter to create an ice-skating rink

Well, we haven't bought any goats, and we passed on the real estate on the moon suggestion. But I like to believe that these employees were engaged! They took the time to share their thoughts, however whimsical, and most of our team members enjoyed a quick laugh thanks to their feedback.

Bottom line: I want our team members to feel like they have a voice, that they can tell us anything they want us to hear!

Best Suggestion

At the end of every year, we select the best of all the suggestions we've received, and pay that contributor $500. I can tell you that these annual awards have paid for themselves many times over. In addition to just raising the level of engagement, these creative suggestions have saved us thousands of dollars in real money.

Here's just one example: Dave, a 10+ year digital press operator for Olympus had an idea. The press he was running was capable of printing white ink, something that not all digital printing presses can do, but we weren't using that capability on this particular press. The maintenance schedule for the press, however, required you to routinely change out the ink, even if it wasn't being used. We were literally throwing away money in unused white ink, until Dave submitted a "Hey Brian!" suggestion to replace the white ink cartridges with a much less expensive head cleaning solution. That idea alone has saved us several thousand dollars.

At the end of the year, I recognized Dave's suggestions in front of all our employees and handed him $500. And while Dave certainly appreciated the money, he also told me that the experience made him feel like he had a real voice in the company, and that he felt empowered to continue to share feedback and suggestions.

Here's another important part of this program. Every suggestion we receive becomes public. We post them in our newsletter and in our lunchroom. As each suggestion is addressed and acted upon, we update the lunchroom list, handwriting *"Done"* and then moving the item to another board. We also update the newsletter list, so our team members have two ways to track our progress. It's worth noting that we post each suggestion anonymously, because we don't want to do anything that might limit participation. But we're always happy when our contributors make their own decision to say: *"That was me!"*

Not all of the feedback we receive is positive. Here are a few other examples of "Hey Brian!" suggestions I've received:

- My manager yells and verbally abuses employees
- I felt a co-worker's feedback was insensitive. It made me feel uncomfortable.
- My manager encouraged me to not report scrap so our scrap rates look better

This sort of feedback is never fun to hear, but it's invaluable. Without this program – and our sincere desire to solicit feedback, positive *or* negative – we might have been oblivious to some very serious issues. This feedback allowed us to investigate and address some very serious concerns.

Roundtable Lunches

Once a month we hold informal, roundtable lunches with small groups of employees. I buy the lunch, and we pay them for their time, my only request is that they speak their minds. We go into these lunches with the hope that they'll drive the topics, because we want it to be all about what's on *their* minds! Sometimes it doesn't start out quite that way, but if it turns out that we're eating in silence, I always have a couple of questions in mind to get the ball rolling. Here are a few of my favorites:

- If you were in my shoes, what one thing would you do differently?
- What do you like least about your job?
- What should we start doing, stop doing or continue doing?

I'm very conscious that my role in these lunches is *facilitator*. I'll do my best to answer any question that is asked of me, although sometimes the answer I choose is "let me get back to you on that" – and I always do, otherwise I lose credibility, right? And while each of these lunches is an opportunity to "push" information out, the main goal is to "pull" feedback in.

First Anniversary Interviews

I've made it a practice to sit down with every employee on their first anniversary with Olympus. I start the conversation by noting the occasion, and thanking them for their contribution over the past year. I tell them that they'll be having a formal review with their direct supervisor, but this is something different. This is just me wanting to know what they think about their job and about the company. Here are some of the questions I like to ask:

- What do you like most about your job?
- What do you enjoy least about your job?
- If you could make one change to your job, what would it be?
- If you owned the company, what's one thing you would do differently?
- Do we have any dumb rules?
- How can I help you do your job better?
- What benefit or perk do you enjoy the most? What benefit or perk do you wish we offered?
- If you won the lottery, what would you do with the money?
- What questions do you have for me?

I hope you'll recognize the importance of that last question. I've come to realize that the other questions *start* the engagement, but the last one often takes it to another level. I have some things I want to know. Isn't it reasonable to expect that the employee will have some things that he or she wants to know? I get to drive the first part of the interview with my questions, but with the last one, I'm handing the keys over to the employee.

Remember, this is all about giving employees a voice. There is voice (lower case) which comes with the invitation to answer the boss's questions. Then there is VOICE (upper case) which comes with the invitation to ask questions of your own. Like I said, that can take this engagement to a whole other level.

Exit Interviews (Real and Hypothetical)

We do exit interviews as a matter of course. If an employee is leaving Olympus, we want to know why. Is it something benign, like a retirement, or maybe one spouse leaving us because the other spouse got a great job in another city? Or, is it something that indicates a problem at Olympus? Either way, we want to give that person the opportunity to make us better. The questions are essentially the same as the First Anniversary interview, just phrased in the past tense. (What *did* you like best about your job? How *could* I have helped you to do your job better?)

We also do "hypothetical" exit interviews. The seed for this actually came as a suggestion from a "real" exit interview. "You know," the employee told me, "if we'd had this conversation a couple of months ago, I might not be leaving." As you can imagine, that was an eye-opener!

As you can also probably imagine, a "hypothetical" exit interview can be weird. It's more like a "role-play" exercise than a real-life situation, and not everyone has the ability to put themselves into a "what if?" mindset. Dave and I talked about this once, because he uses role-play extensively in his sales training. He observed that it's hard to predict who's going to engage well enough to provide a worthwhile experience, and I have definitely found that to be true. But I think more depends on the interviewer than the interviewee.

The key is to make the employee comfortable. I start out by telling them that I know I'm putting them in a weird situation. I stress that I'm *not* doing it because I think they're unhappy and thinking about leaving. I'm doing it because I want to make sure that they *are* happy and planning on staying!

Here are some of the questions I've asked:

- Do we as a company do anything that keeps you from doing your job the way you think it should be done?
- Do you think we've hired any losers lately? I'm not asking you for names, just whether you think we've made any hiring mistakes!
- What set of circumstances would make you say *this place is going downhill*?
- What set of circumstances would make you say *I hate this place*?
- Have you seen or heard or felt any of those circumstances lately, even a little bit?

So Brian, you may be thinking, how do you decide when you need to do one of these "hypothetical" exit interviews. The answer is that sometimes it's pretty random. I'll sometimes run into someone on the shop floor and think that he or she is a good candidate for this particular conversation.

Other times, though, it's because someone – maybe me, or more likely, a team-member's direct supervisor – catches just a hint of something less-than-ideal going on. Doctors talk about early detection, and that's what we try to do, catching problems when they're small and more easily treatable. Once you get to the point where someone is *fully* unhappy and *planning* on leaving, you're probably looking at a real exit interview before too long.

****

By the way, the "Dave" I mentioned a couple of paragraphs ago was Dave my co-author, not Dave the press operator at Olympus. But, speaking of Dave my co-author…

4 Back To Advertising
Dave Fellman

Brian and I had a very short conversation about how to structure this book. We both like to write in the first person – "I" and "We" – but the "We" is mostly not about he and me. For Brian, it's about he and his team. For me, it's about me and my clients. Plus, he's the people guy and I'm the sales guy, and so far, we've been trying to stick to our own principal areas of expertise. So what we decided to do was go back and forth, and to tell you just below each chapter heading who's writing what.

"I hope that won't be confusing," I said.

"It won't be any more confusing than any normal day for a typical small business owner or manager," he answered. "We all go back and forth all day, right? This is just back and forth between two of the many "hats" most of us wear."

So, having said all of that, I'm now going to write something about *employee* engagement. One of my clients has an interesting variation on the "giving employees a voice" theme. She sits down with each new employee after 30 days on the job for a "fill in the blanks" exercise. It has four elements:

I want you to _____
I need you to _____
I depend on you to _____
I trust you to _____

She has found that she has to walk most employees through the subtle differences between *want, need, depend on* and *trust*, but she has also found it to be a worthwhile exercise, because it creates a much deeper understanding of each employee's *hierarchy of needs*.

She readily admits, by the way, that she borrowed that term from the psychologist, Abraham Maslow, and that it means something far more complex in Maslow's usage. In hers, it's simply a matter of a better understanding of what it will take to manage and motivate an individual most effectively.

It's not just a matter of the employee's wants and needs, though. The second stage of this exercise turns the table on the employee. *My client* fills in the same blanks, in other words, communicating her expectations to the employee. Now, both parties are better positioned to understand where the other one is coming from.

The third stage is to revisit this conversation from time to time. Sometimes that involves a promotion, or some other change in job description. It can also involve a life-change situation, for example, a birth or death or marriage or divorce. Sometimes it's just a matter of checking to see if anything has changed since the last conversation.

Engagement is all about communication, right? Here's another good word: *Transparent*. I found this 4-part definition in the Merriam Webster dictionary:

a: free from pretense or deceit
b: easily detected or seen through
c: readily understood
d: characterized by visibility or accessibility of information especially concerning business practices

All four relate to this conversation, but I think one does much more so than the others. *Readily understood*. Let me remind you of something I wrote all the way back in the Introduction: *Real communication requires that both the sender and the receiver connect all the dots. This is critically important, because it's possible to have 100% engagement even if you don't have 100% communication. I can be fully engaged and onboard with what I think you said, right? But that might take us anywhere between 1° and 180° off course.*

Engagement is all about communication! Communication is all about transparency, defined as being readily understood.

****

OK, back in Chapter 1, I was writing about the three stages of suspect engagement, specifically with static advertising. The first stage is to capture attention. The second stage is to establish interest. The third stage is to motivate action. Now don't forget, you'll only get action if the second stage is satisfied – establishment of interest. Also, don't forget that you don't *want* action from anyone who really isn't interested! This is a process of separating *likely suspects* from *people who will never buy from you*. The overall goal is to apply most of your engagement resources to the situations that are most likely to provide a return on your investment.

This is especially important in any situation where a *salesperson* will have to engage with a suspect in order to make the sale. A funnel makes a good analogy here. The wide mouth of the funnel is the advertising program – for example, the newspaper ad that our fictional fitness club is running to its universe of 25,000 suspects. The narrow stem of the funnel is The Point of Sale. The result we're hoping for is a steady flow of qualified prospects. So here's a question, what's the Worst Case Scenario?

The obvious worst result would be zero responses. But equally as bad might be a torrent of tire-kickers. It's entirely possibly to plug up the stem of a sales funnel with people who take up a lot of time and never buy. On one hand, that's part of the risk – part of the game! You can't sell to everyone, even the *fully qualified prospects* who engage with you at The Point of Sale.

On the other hand, time is money, and time/money spent on tire-kickers is generally not a great investment.

Call, Click or Visit

Part of the solution to this problem lies in the action you hope to motivate. In the modern world, *call, click or visit* has become a common catchphrase. But here's my question, do you want them to *call*, or *click*, or *visit*? First, decide. Then make it clear in your ad which response you desire.

Let's look at some of the plusses and minuses of each response option. If you ask for a call, you might change the level of engagement from *static advertisement* to *qualifying conversation*, and possibly even to *making the sale*. If you ask for a click, you can hopefully get people to visit your website, where you can tell them much more about what's for sale. If you ask for a visit, you might even draw them directly to The Point of Sale.

On the minus side, a call or a visit can come at an inconvenient time for you. And a click to your website might limit your opportunity to follow up.

Into The Store

Let's go back for a moment to our discussion of the purpose of advertising. And let's draw a distinction between "retail" and "commercial" sales. This is related to B2C vs. B2B, but that's not a perfect equivalency. The main difference between retail and commercial is that retail implies a store. So let's take the next step. *The purpose of retail advertising is to get people into the store.*

I wrote earlier that you should engage each category differently – suspects, prospects, customers and maximized customers. That still holds true, but it's probably less critical for a purely retail business. For example, *EVERYTHING'S ON SALE!* is an advertising message that might well draw suspects, prospects and customers into – or back into – a store.

Now let's draw another distinction. Some stores are more about buying than selling. I used restaurants earlier as an example of this. Convenience stores are another example. You go in with the expectation of buying something off a shelf, or out of a cooler or freezer.

The most likely personal engagement occurs when you reach the cash register to pay for your purchases. The second most likely engagement occurs if you have to ask someone where you might find a particular product. The least likely personal engagement tends to be a greeting or a sincere thank you. Yes, that's a direct criticism of most of my visits to convenience stores!

It's not fair, though, to accuse convenience stores of being the only ones guilty of this particular crime. I walk into far too many places of business where the greeting is perfunctory at best. In fact, the tone of voice or body language I encounter at "first contact" often makes me think they're thinking: "Oh crap, another customer!" And I walk out of far too many businesses feeling like the money I just spent wasn't appreciated. (In fact, I've been known to walk out of businesses *without* spending money when I didn't feel like the *opportunity* to do business with me was appreciated!)

The *greeting* is important to your engagement strategy. The *expression of appreciation* is important to your engagement strategy. So here's a challenge. On a scale of 1-10, give yourself a rating on how well you and your team execute the greeting stage. On the same scale, give yourself and your team a rating on how well you execute the "thank you" stage. And then on the same scale, rate your confidence in how well you really know what's going on, every day, with every employee, and every person who walks into your store.

More than anything else, this is an exercise in honesty and objectivity. If you think you're doing all of this well, but you really are not, the whole foundation of your business is flawed. There's almost nothing that's more dangerous than to *think* you have loyal and happy customers when the reality is more like 80% of your customers feeling 80% good about you. Sure, that's a *level* of happy and loyal, but is it as high as you want it?

I've strayed from the topic of advertising, I know, but this does all tie together. A few paragraphs back, I suggested that the Worst Case Scenario might be for your advertising to generate a torrent of tire kickers. The real WCS might be for your advertising to generate a steady flow of qualified prospects and then you blow it at the Point of Sale, where *advertising engagement* turns into *personal engagement*. It's been said that you only get one chance to make a first impression. The truth is that commerce usually puts you in a "developing" situation where you must *make and maintain* a good impression throughout the engagement process.

And by the way, that's as true of an *office* as it is of a *store,* and it's true for a phone call as well as a physical visit.

****

Brian jumping in here. I agree completely with Dave about the importance of an effective and meaningful greeting – and the importance of demonstrating your appreciation in a retail, point of sale setting. Just a week or so ago, I ordered a cup of coffee at my favorite coffee shop. The person behind the counter – Dave would say *salesperson* – looked me in the eye and asked me: "How's your morning going?"

Between the eye engagement and the tone of voice, it felt very sincere. And after my answer, and placing my order, she said: "We're on it. We're going to make you a great cup of coffee. Have a great day." It was simple and meaningful. I left the store feeling like she – and therefore *they* – really appreciated my business.

I don't remember how much I paid for this cup of coffee, nor did I care, then or now. I drive out of my way to go to this coffee shop, because I feel like the employees care about their mission, and if they care, that means I get a good cup of coffee, right?

And, of course*, greeting* and *expression of appreciation* go beyond the retail environment. I'd argue that there's just as much value in ensuring that these exist in office environments, and in B2B engagements. B2B may appear to be more *transactional* –- you need supplies for your office, find the lowest price and buy. But I run a B2B company, and while it's true that we've never come face-to-face with most of our customers and suppliers, and only communicate with many of them via phone or email, it's still true that we all like to buy from people we like. It's simply more enjoyable to do business with pleasant people, who make us feel like we matter and show that they care. So make it your business, even on a phone call or email, to demonstrate that level of engagement with the people you do business with.

Let's face it, unless you've developed something completely new, something that doesn't exist anywhere else in the market, odds are that your competitors can produce the exact same product. I know that our competitors operate similar equipment, and that they're calling on the same people we're calling on. So what makes the difference between getting the business and not?

This is another area in which we engage with our customers. *"Why did you/do you choose Olympus?"* It's worth mentioning, I think, that we have two fairly distinct groups of customers. On the printing side of our business, we sell a custom manufactured product, and it's very much a *relationship* sale. On the flag side, it's much more of a commodity product, and much more of a *transactional* sale. Still, when we ask *why*, we tend to get the same answers from both groups, and it very rarely has anything (or at least *everything*) to do with price.

"We like working with you."

"We trust you. We know if there's an issue, you'll make it right."

Like *and* trust. That's a pretty good combination, right? But I want you to think about whether one works without the other. I also want you to think about how simple this really is. Show that you care, through *greeting, expression of appreciation* and *standing behind your work.* All of that adds up to be a significant differentiator, because *not everyone does it!*

One more thing about being nice and showing that you care. It adds absolutely nothing to your cost of sales! Not a dime! But like Dave says, you need to *know* that all of this is being done and done well in your company. I strongly urge you to go back a few pages and take his 1-10 challenge!

****

Into The Store In The Modern World

Thanks, Brian. OK, back to advertising engagement. *The purpose of retail advertising is to get people into the store.* That raises two questions. First, what defines a store? Does it have to be brick-and-mortar? In the modern world, it absolutely does not. In 2018, according to Forbes Magazine, Walmart, Amazon and CVS were the 1-2-3 largest retailers in the world. Amazon added some brick-and-mortar when it acquired Whole Foods in 2017. Walmart and CVS have long had their huge physical presence, but they have also become major players in e-commerce. The store is where you go to buy – or to be sold to – and that's true whether it's made of whole atoms or just electrons.

Second question: What is the purpose of *commercial* advertising? As noted earlier, this is related to B2B vs. B2C, but that's not a perfect equivalency. *Commercial*, at least for the purposes of this book, is more about selling that happens away from a retail environment.

Before I go any further, I'd better deal with another "opposite" of retail. In addition to retail vs. commercial, there's also the distinction between retail vs. wholesale. The Merriam-Webster dictionary defines retail as *the sale of commodities or goods in small quantities to ultimate consumers*. It defines wholesale as *the sale of commodities in quantity, usually for resale (as by a retail merchant)*. In other words, wholesalers supply retailers who sell to end users, typically through a store.

A retail sale may involve a salesperson, although the role of that salesperson usually tends more toward customer service – providing information and collecting payment – than toward convincing. A commercial sale almost always involves a salesperson, in a role that may range from providing information to "closing the sale." Retail typically involves payment at The Point of Sale. Commercial more typically involves invoicing and credit terms.

It's worth noting, I think, that the salesperson in the commercial sale might be "inside" or "outside." In fact, many companies utilize a combination of inside and outside sales. I do want to draw a distinction between salespeople and order-takers, but I'll come back to that later on.

For now, let's go back to that second question, and answer it this way: *The purpose of commercial advertising is to get people into the funnel,* where a salesperson can engage, qualify and hopefully succeed at turning suspects into customers.

Free From Limitation

The three stages I wrote about earlier still apply to the commercial advertising process: *capture attention, establish interest, motivate action*. The action options are also still the same: *call, click or visit*. Here, though, is an important point. In the modern world – the modern *commercial* world – *click* and *visit* probably involve the same destination, the advertiser's website.

Let me back up for a moment, though. In retail, The Point of Sale is a store. It can be a virtual store or a brick-and-mortar store, but as I've noted, the purpose of retail advertising is to get people into that store. To put that another way, retail is all about getting buyers to come to you.

Commercial selling is free from that limitation. And *limitation* is exactly the word I want to use! For many years, in my seminars, I've been using a simple graphic example to illustrate this point. Back in the old days, I used to draw a circle on a flip chart, taking up maybe half of the middle of the page. "This represents the people who will come to you," I would say. "They'll find you in the Yellow Pages (remember the Yellow Pages?) or hear about you somehow or maybe just drive by and see your sign. But they'll come to you, without you having to do anything more than you're doing right now."

Then I would draw another, larger shape, taking it all the way to the edges of the page. (These days, of course, I do all of this with animated PowerPoint slides.) Then or now, I would say: "This represents the people who *won't* come to you. That doesn't mean they won't buy from you. But it does mean that you have to do more than you're doing now."

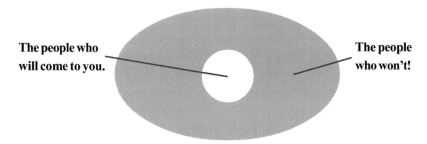

The people who will come to you.   **The people who won't!**

In pure retail, that's limited to advertising. In the commercial environment, it can also be a salesforce that identifies and pursues likely suspects – a far more proactive process!

Process Is Key

Process is the key word here. As one of my old mentors used to say: "Making a sale is a process, not an event." I want to talk more about the selling part of the selling process later on – that defined as the part where the salesperson is actively involved. Right now, we're still talking about advertising, and *call, click or visit*.

What we're really talking about here are *sales leads*. Ask any salesperson this question: *Would you rather make cold calls or follow-up on qualified leads?* The answer is almost certain to be *leads*, with one caveat. Most salespeople will also tell you that most "qualified" leads are anything but. Having said that, it's definitely more desirable when a buyer finds his or her own way to the funnel, without the salesperson having to go through the initial stages of pursuit.

Thirty years ago, the goal of most commercial advertising was "to make the phones ring." If attention was captured and interest was established, the funnel was usually entered via a phone call. Depending on the product or service or company, an "inside" salesperson might carry the ball. Alternately, the *lead* might be passed along to an "outside" salesperson.

Just as with retail advertising, if a call is what you want, make that clear in your advertising. The question is whether you're better off asking for a different action? As I mentioned, *click* or *visit* in commercial advertising probably involves the same destination, your website. And in my view of the modern commercial sales process, that's where you want your suspects to enter your funnel!

Suspects and Inquiries

Why is that? Well, let's remember the difference between suspects and prospects. *They are suspects when you think they might be prospects!* Might be! You also have to consider the possibility that they're tire-kickers, or simply not qualified in some other way.

Do you remember "bingo cards" – which were more formally called *reader service cards*? I'm talking about post cards, which were either bound in or just placed inside the pages of a magazine. Both consumer magazines and trade publications used to make very heavy use of this "enhanced" advertising strategy.

The way it worked was ingenious on several levels. First, you could usually buy an ad in the magazine without also buying space on the bingo card. If you did that, your ad shouldered the whole load of engagement – capturing attention, establishing interest and motivating action.

For a little more money, you could also buy space on the bingo card, which carried the return address of the publisher, and typically listed multiple advertisers. The reader could indicate which advertiser(s) he or she was interested in, provide contact information, and simply mail the card back to the publisher, usually postage-free. The publisher would then issue a "lead report" to each advertiser for appropriate follow up.

For a higher price, you could buy an individual response card with your own return address, bypassing the publisher and theoretically speeding up the whole inquiry-and-follow-up process.

This was all oriented toward making it easy for the reader to engage and take action. But does *easy* mean *serious*? Does *inquiry* mean *fully qualified prospect*? I remember a conversation with a client who was contemplating an individual response card in a trade magazine. They'd participated in the bingo card program in the past and been happy with the *quantity* of response. At the same time, they were not-at-all-satisfied with the *quality*. They'd sent out hundreds of packages of information and samples in response to these sales leads, and received only a small number of orders.

Now, part of the problem was what I would consider an inappropriate follow-up response – although it might be more correct to use the word *insufficient*. They received inquiries and sent out information and samples, but they didn't take responsibility to engage beyond that. They left it up to the suspect to take the next step, which is usually bad strategy.

The client was convinced, though, that a bigger problem was the lag time between inquiry and follow-up. By the time the information arrived, these were "cold" leads. "We need to strike while the iron is hot," she told me." I said, "OK, but let's do one more thing to see if we can qualify just how 'hot' these leads are. Let's *not* do a postage paid response card. Let's make them put on a stamp."

If I remember correctly, a post card stamp cost $.24 back then. Not a lot of money, right? But in theory, the cost of the stamp and the act of having to place it on the card would slow down the process for at least some of the tire-kickers. Remember, this is still all about putting your engagement resources into situations where you're most likely to get a good return on your investment!

Also remember that there's a cost attached to the follow-up. In this case, the package of information and samples represented almost $5.00 of real material cost, plus another $1.00 for postage. All of that has to be part of the *investment tolerance* equation!

I'm not saying that you should skimp on your investment. Quite the opposite, I usually come down on the side of *more* rather than *less*. But I always come down on the side of *wise* investment!

Engaging With Your Website

It's been quite a long time since I've used a bingo card. Just yesterday, though, I responded to a *call, click or visit* advertisement by *visiting* the company's website. And when I got there, I found:

1. A TV commercial
2. A complete catalog of the company's products
3. A collection of product reviews and testimonials
4. A way to make a purchase
5. An incentive to make a purchase immediately

To put that differently, I found myself in a store, and you might even call it an *enhanced* store. The combination of video, text and graphics provided a lot of information, and the eCommerce page offered me a "first-time-buyer" discount and a simple and straightforward ordering process.

But as it turned out, I didn't make a purchase, basically because I couldn't figure out which of this company's products was best suited to my application. Yes, there was a lot of information, but it didn't answer my questions. I still needed more help.

Two Stories

I spoke at a Sales Leadership conference a few years ago, and I sat in on all of the presentations before my 11:00 AM time slot. The 9:00 AM speaker was the most interesting of the three, mostly because he walked out on stage and announced that: "Selling is over. Salespeople are no longer required. Anyone who wants anything can just go online and find whatever they need with no human intervention. Sorry, folks, but that's the way it is!"

I remember my first thought: "Who invited this guy?" But I listened as he expanded on his opening statements, and found that I agreed with much of what he had to say. He used Barnes and Noble as an example of an enterprise in which no salespeople are required. Now, I've already noted that many retail businesses are more about buying than selling. I have certainly exchanged currency for merchandise with human clerks at Barnes and Noble stores – in fact, before eBooks, that was one of my favorite things to do! Even now, I purchase most of my eBooks at barnesandnoble.com without any human interaction.

Here's another story, though, which also reflects a retail situation. I bought a new desk some years back, and I wanted to set it up facing outward into the room. This was pre-Bluetooth, so it meant dealing with all of the various cords and wires connected to my keyboard, mouse, monitor, telephone, etc., and unlike many "modern" desks, this one didn't have pre-cut holes. No big deal, I thought, I'll just drill myself a hole.

I measured all of the cords and wires and determined that I'd need a 1½ inch diameter hole, and since I didn't have a drill bit that big, I headed off to Ace Hardware. There I found a confusing array of drill bits and hole saws, ranging in price from $6.98 to $19.95. I narrowed my choice down to three, but that's as far as I could get on my own, so I was pretty happy when a salesperson came around the corner, into my aisle.

"How can I help you today?" he asked.

I told him: "I need a large drill bit, but I'm not sure which of these is the right one."

"OK," he said, "I can help you with that, but let's start here…you don't really need a drill bit."

I said: "Oh really?"

"No sir," he said. "What you actually need is a hole."

He was right of course. And then he said: "OK, first question…how big a hole do you need?"

"It needs to be an inch and a half wide," I told him.

"OK," he said. "So far, so good. Any of these three bits will drill you a one-and-a-half inch hole. Now, what do you need this hole drilled in?"

"My desk," I told him.

"OK," he said. "What's your desk made of, wood or metal?"

"Wood," I said. Then he asked: "Is it solid wood, or could it be a laminate material over pressboard?"

"That's what it is," I said. "Laminate over pressboard."

"OK," he said, "next question: How thick is the part of the desk you need the hole through?"

"Maybe an inch or an inch-and-a-quarter," I said.

"All right," he said. "Only one more question. How many of these holes are you gonna need?"

"Just one," I said. "I just want to be able to keep all the wires from my computer and my phone out of sight as much as possible."

"Yeah," he said, "that can be pretty messy with all them wires hanging out all over your desk. OK, this bit right here is the one you want for the hole you need." He handed me one of three products I'd been looking at — interestingly, it was the least expensive of the three.

He seemed to sense that I'd appreciate a little bit more explanation. "If you'd needed your hole in something made of metal," he said, "you'd have had to buy this one here," — the most expensive of the three — "and if you'd needed to drill a lot of holes in wood or pressboard, I'd have recommended this one," — which cost almost as much — "but the one you got there will drill you one hole through inch or inch-and-a-quarter pressboard without any problem, and if you need another hole or two just like it, any time in the future, you ought to be able to count on that bit for those holes too."

I thanked him for his help, and then I asked: "Have you ever had any sales training?"

"Gosh, no," he said. "I'm not any kind of salesman, I'm just a clerk in a store."

Yeah, maybe. Or maybe he's the ultimate example of an engaging and consultative salesperson.

How Can I Help You?

There's one more thing I want to mention before I go back to advertising engagement. Well, maybe two or three things. The first is the way this salesperson handled the *greeting* stage. As I've noted, the tone of voice or body language I encounter at "first contact" with retail employees often makes me think they're thinking "Oh crap, another customer!" They don't say that, of course, but that's often the way I perceive them when they ask: "Can I help you?"

This salesperson seemed to be operating on the assumption that he *could* help me, the only question was *how*? So that's how he greeted me: "How can I help you today?" Add in the smile on his face, and I would grade that a 10 on a scale of 10 in terms of greeting/engagement technique.

"Can I help you?" with a warm, welcoming smile might earn a 9 on a scale of 10.

"Can I help you?" without the smile might earn a 7, or maybe even a 6.

"What can I do for you?" even with a smile would only earn a 5 in my book. Would you agree that there's a difference between *do* and *help*?

Would you also agree that little things can make big differences?

Ace Is The Place

The second thing I want to mention is the brilliance of Ace's advertising tagline. It used to be: "Ace is the place with the helpful hardware man." Now it's been modified to: "Ace is the place with the helpful hardware pro." I suspect that the initial reasoning for that change was to remove any hint of gender bias, but I think they get an added boost from the term *pro*. *Helpful* plus *professional* is a very strong combination, especially when faced with the sort of competition Ace Hardware has to deal with every day.

As you may know, Ace is a franchise, but as such, it can still be considered "locally owned." It's chief local competition comes from the big box stores like Lowes and Home Depot. It's probably fair to say that those companies employ helpful and professional people as well, but I think Ace has established greater "ownership" of that feature through its *branding*. (More on that term a little farther along.)

Ace also faces online competition. I would bet that there's *something* Ace sells that you can't buy on Amazon, but offhand I don't know what it would be.

So why go to Ace, as opposed to Lowes or Home Depot or Amazon or any other option? I go there when I need more information – more help! – than I can get online. I also tend to go there when time is an issue, because Ace always seems to be overstaffed while the big boxes always seem understaffed.

Wait! That's probably not fair. The truth of the matter is that both Ace and the big boxes are usually *correctly* staffed – for their business model! Brian wrote earlier about *purpose* and *Core Values*. It seems obvious that one of Ace Hardware's Core Values is to invest in people – both *quality* and *quantity* – to make sure that every customer experiences a Helpful Hardware Pro without having to wait too long for attention. They probably operate with a higher payroll as a percentage of sales than the big boxes do, but I suspect that's by design.

 Brian also pointed me toward Ace Hardware's Vision Statement: "To be the best, most helpful hardware stores on the planet." We both think they nailed it!

Final Thing

The final thing I want to mention about my Ace Hardware experience is this. I engaged with a salesperson who didn't think of himself as a salesperson, but who did a very professional job of selling nonetheless. He may never have heard terms like *needs assessment, consultative selling*, and *applications product knowledge*, but he managed to create a very positive buying experience for his customer.

Did he generate revenue, which is the Prime Directive for any business? Yes, although it was only $6.98. Did he generate any *additional* revenue? Not in the sense that I spent more than I had to or intended to that day, but the positive buying experience he created has brought me back to that Ace Hardware store many times.

Thinking back on that day, though, I wonder if he couldn't have generated some additional revenue. He did ask me if there was anything else I needed, but he didn't offer anything suggestive. With the power of hindsight, I'm going to suggest the following scenario:

"What kind of shape is your drill in?" he might have asked me. "Is it corded or cordless? Would you like to look at some of the new cordless drills that are 2-3 times more powerful than the first generation of battery powered drills?" I'm not sure I would have bought a new drill that day, but I'm not sure I wouldn't have either!

The point is this, you should always be thinking about maximizing the value of each engagement. As noted, we're going to be talking about *customer maximization* in a later chapter. Part of that can be accomplished by maximizing each engagement – but with caution! It's certainly possible to make a good first impression and then blow it with a bad finish.

This, I think, points to the difference between *upselling* and *cross-selling*.

My Helpful Hardware Pro didn't try to *upsell* me to something more than I needed, and I appreciated that. But he did miss out on an opportunity to *cross-sell* me, or to put that differently, to *educate* me about something else that I could buy from him if I had a want or need for it.

Do You Want Fries With That?

The most famous example of "suggestive" selling in our time is probably: "Do you want fries with that?" I think you'll probably agree that most people don't *need* the fries, but those six words have sold a lot of potatoes! So here's a question. Does "suggestive" selling – cross-selling – represent *added value*, or simply business greed?

Here's an answer, in the form of another story. This may have been 25 years ago, and I was driving from my home in Cary, NC to Kill Devil Hills, which is out on North Carolina's Outer Banks. I left just before 6:00 PM after a full day in the office, and I was scheduled to meet with a client at 8:00 the next morning. The weather was marginal to miserable for about the first two-thirds of my 200 mile drive, and construction and an accident turned what's normally a 3+ hour drive into a 5+ hour ordeal. I was grumpy and tired when I pulled into Plymouth, NC just after 10:00 PM, with at least another hour to go. I needed coffee, and the only thing open in town was McDonald's.

I parked, walked in, and ordered a large coffee. The server, a woman about my age, poured it and put the top on and then smiled sort of sweetly at me. "You know what would be really good with this?" she said. "A little box of our McCookies. Would you like one of those?"

Now when I think McDonald's, I don't think about cookies. I guess I knew that they sold them, with that knowledge stored somewhere in the back of my mind, but I certainly didn't walk in there that night expecting to buy any. When I did think about cookies, though, my whole outlook changed. "Yes," I thought, "I *would* like some of those," so I ordered them, paid for them, walked back out to my car and opened the little box. The next 10-15 minutes was the best part of my drive, and I owed that to another salesperson who probably never thought of herself as a salesperson, but who did a very professional selling job nonetheless.

She engaged with me. She generated revenue — *additional revenue!* —

for her employer. Beyond that, I received *added value*. That's the essence of win-win selling, right? And yes, it's probably true that most upselling and a lot of cross-selling is mostly motivated by business greed, but there are also times when the suggestion is appreciated. I think it's probably worth *asking* just about everybody if they might *want* something else that you sell, just to be sure that you don't miss anybody who would value the suggestion!

Salesperson vs. Order Taker

As I mentioned earlier, I want to draw a distinction between *salespeople* and *order-takers*. This may be mostly *sales snobbery* on my part, but as I also mentioned earlier, some people consider selling an honorable profession – which by definition must mean that it's conducted by professionals! In the sales community, *professionalism* has three main components: knowledge, integrity and convincing skills.

An "inside" salesperson may only need two of those. Sometimes it's not about convincing, it's just about taking the order! And there's nothing wrong with that! In fact, there are times when all an "outside" salesperson has to do is take the order.

But as I hope you'll see from these two stories, there are also times when even "inside" sales rises to a higher level of *professionalism*. I love it when that happens!

Back To Your Website

OK, let's go back to the idea of *click/visit* and my statement that your website should be the place where you want commercial suspects to enter your funnel – and also possibly where you want retail suspects to enter your store.

Let's consider three scenarios. First, your product or service can be easily purchased online, so your website is a full-fledged store, all the way from providing information to money changing hands. Second, your product or service can be purchased online, but options and/or other issues make that more complex. Third, your product or service can't be purchased online. It's just too customized and/or complex.

In the first scenario, the ratio between *store* and *funnel entry* might be 80/20. In the second, it might be 20/80. In the third, it's 0/100. (Remember, in the third scenario – and probably the second scenario too – you *want* a salesperson involved.)

No matter which scenario applies to your business, though, I have the same first question: *How does your website greet each visitor?*

Here are three things to consider in answering that question:

1. *Does your website make a good first impression?* Just as with static advertising, I'm talking about words and images.
2. *Does your website* connect *to whatever advertising brought people to it?* Again, this is about words and images. It's also about *consistency* of colors and style. And maybe the most important parts this *graphic design* element are your name and logo. The goal here is for people to recognize immediately that they've arrived at the place where you and they were hoping they would get to.
3. *Does your website make it clear and easy how to take the next step, and give you everything you need to take* your *next step?* This is where the three scenarios diverge. In the "mostly" retail scenario, the next step is probably information and eCommerce for a specific product. (*eCommerce* in this application simply means *order and pay*.) In the "partly" retail scenario, it's all of that plus how to engage to get more help. In the commercial scenario, it's information plus how to engage to get more help *plus* all of the information *you will need* in order to follow up.

The third question takes us back to a comment I made earlier, about the plusses and minuses of call, click or visit. *A click to your website might limit your opportunity to follow up.* Let's couple that with some very fundamental sales knowledge: *Commercial selling is all about follow-up!*

Now it's true that not every retail engagement results in an immediate sale. It's also true that some commercial engagements *do* result in an immediate sale. So maybe I should state my point this way*: If you don't make an* immediate *sale, but you still hope to make an* eventual *sale, you must continue the engagement – in other words, follow up!*

So what will you need to know in order to continue the engagement? You may remember the Five W's from back in your school days, sometimes referred to as the Five W's and How, or 5W1H? In order of importance, you need to know *who, where, what, why, when* and *how.*

Hopefully the *who* is pretty obvious. But beyond simply capturing a name, I hope you'll also see the value in learning the person's title/responsibilities? It can be very helpful, at this point, to know whether you're dealing with a likely decision-maker – as opposed to someone with a "lesser" role in the research-and-buy process.

The *where* may seem less obvious in terms of importance, until I explain that I'm talking about *where* this person can be found so that you can follow up. *Where* might include a company name, a street or mailing address, a phone number, an e-mail address or even a social media handle – or maybe better still, all of the above!

What, why and *when* tend to go together – *what* they're interested in and *why,* and *when* they need it. The *what* may be obvious, especially if you have a limited product line. The *why* and *when* can make all of the difference in the world when it comes down to closing the sale. Consider these three scenarios:

- I might be interested in (what you sell).
- I need to replace a broken (what you sell).
- I need to replace a broken (what you sell) and it's critically important to my business!

I'm not trying to say that the first scenario is any less valid or important than the third. What I am trying to say is that it's less *urgent.* And I can't say for sure that the third scenario represents a *fully qualified* lead, although it looks pretty good on the surface. In other words, it sure looks like a *hot* lead.

It's also worth considering that *when* can have two meanings, one of which is more important than the other. The less important *when* is the day/ time of the inquiry, which really only provides a baseline for measuring response time. The more important *when* is the point in time at which they need whatever it is they came looking for, and that can range from "more information" to the product or service itself.

I think *how* in this particular application refers to a preferred means of follow-up. But that begs a question, *whose preference*? Is it good strategy to let suspects tell you how to take your next step? If, say, a call or an email would work equally well for you, then I'm all for asking the suspect's preference. But if you're pretty sure that a phone call is better selling strategy, I say go ahead and make the call.

Millennials

Speaking of follow-up phone calls, I have been told that selling to Millennials is very frustrating, because they don't want to talk, they only want to text or tweet or email, and that's not as direct as face-to-face – or at least voice-to-voice – engagement. I hear this mostly from Boomers (like myself) and Gen X'ers who now represent the "old guard" in commerce. What's interesting is that I remember us Boomers and the Greatest Generation who preceded us complaining about the X'ers, and I'm pretty sure the GG's complained about my generation in concert with the generation that preceded them.

Everything changes. That would seem to leave you with two choices. You can change with the times, or you can defend your position. Thankfully, there's a third choice. You can do both! But let me come back to that. For now, I seem to have raised another "people" issue, which means it's time to give the ball back to Brian.

With a question: *Do you find the Millennials in your company to be especially challenging?*

5 Increasing Engagement
Brian Adam

Do I find the Millennials in my company to be especially challenging?

That's a great question Dave. The short answer is *no* – every generation presents management challenges, but I enjoy working with Millennials, and we have some great ones on our team. For the record I was born in 1978, so technically I'm on the back end of Generation X, but only a couple of years away from being a Millennial myself.

There's definitely a lot of buzz on this topic in management discussions, about Millennials and the impact they're having on our workplace. Millennials now represent the largest population in the workforce in the United States. That means the companies that best engage and embrace Millennials will have a competitive advantage in the marketplace, especially over others who ignore or don't adapt to this generation.

As I'm writing this, in the 4th Quarter of 2019, the job market is hot as well. There are lots of "alternate" employment opportunities for everyone. That's all going to change in about 5 months, when Covid-19 hits, but we don't know that yet. We do know that it's important to engage this particular demographic. The goal is to ensure that (a) we're providing a place where people will want to work, and (b) all of our team members are contributing to our success.

Let's start by taking a look at some common traits that apply to ALL Millennials:

- They all live in their parent's basements
- They have no work ethic – a very lazy generation!
- They feel entitled – they love participation trophies and they don't believe in competition

- They're impatient – they believe in a maximum tenure of 6 months at any one place of employment
- Their only form of communication is Snapchat & Twitter – at all costs, they avoid speaking to other human beings
- Thanks to Spellcheck, they never learned how to spell

Now, I don't believe any of that, but these attributes are commonly used to describe the Millennials. Most of them are blatantly false, and some are outright ridiculous – mythology not reality.

Here's The Reality

I believe that Millennials are actually more similar to other generations than they are different. Most of the Millennials I know – and work with – share *these* attributes:

- They want to be given interesting work to do
- They want to be empowered to make decisions
- They want to be rewarded on the basis of their performance
- They want to be given the chance to advance
- They want to have their opinions and feedback heard

Is all of that really that different from the Baby Boomers or Gen Xers? Who wouldn't want interesting work to do? Who doesn't want to be empowered, to be rewarded or to have the opportunity to advance and be heard? I believe that when it comes to management in general – and especially employee engagement – the best practices apply pretty consistently to all of the generations in today's workforce.

How Are Millennials Different?

While Millennials share many similarities to the other generations, there are a couple of noteworthy differences. If you understand and address these differences, it can have a huge impact on your ability to keep your Millennials engaged.

First, understand that Millennials tend not to be afraid to change jobs. Treat them poorly or disrespect them and they'll likely be posting their resume on

Indeed within the hour. In a recent survey conducted by Gallup, 63% of Millennials believe it is "very likely" or "somewhat likely" that they would find a job as good as the one they have if they were let go. Millennials are certainly not afraid of jumping ship.

Millennials can be "impatient." They are less likely to "put in their time." Want to scare off a millennial? Tell them they have to wait 3-5 years to be eligible for a promotion. And I'm perfectly OK with this mindset. Why should it matter how long someone has worked? If they're ready, qualified, and the best candidate for a position, promote them now. Most entrepreneurs are impatient (myself included). I think we can harness Millennials' impatience to drive change.

Next, understand that Millennials want work with a purpose. Yes, we all want purpose in what we do, but Millennials are far less likely to work "only" for a paycheck. They want their company – and their role within their company – to mean something; to stand for some greater good.

Finally, Millennials value different benefits and perks than other generations. Baby Boomers and Generation Xers tend to place a high value on lifestyle perks – health insurance, paid vacation and retirement plans. Millennials tend to value perks that offer them greater flexibility and those related to children and education. They're also far more likely to leave a company for a perk than any other generation.

According to a recent Gallup survey, 50% of Millennials say they would switch to a job that allows them to work part time, and 37% would switch to a job that allows them to work off-site part of the time. As a printer, I struggle with that one, because we need on-site work because that's where all the equipment is. Still, it's important to note that Millennials place a high value on work/life balance.

A "Typical" Millennial

I had lunch recently with "Julie" – a customer of ours who happens to a be Millennial.

Brian: "How's your new role going?"
Julie: "It's OK, but it's not really what I thought it would be."
Brian: "You seem pretty frustrated. What's going on?"

Julie: "Our company doesn't care about us. They treat us like a number."
Brian: "Uh-oh. What happened?"
Julie: "They sent out an email, telling us they were tracking our hours, and would be following up with anyone who showed up after 8:00 AM, took an extended lunch break, or left before 5:00 PM."
Brian: "Sounds like someone was abusing some freedom, and they're trying to ensure that all the employees are putting in their time."
Julie: "Exactly. But I live 45 miles from the office. Traffic is unpredictable. With my baby due in 3 months, I'm not sure I want to work for someone with such rigid policies. I get my work done, but I know there will be days where I need to leave early or come in late."
Brian: "It sounds to me like, instead of addressing the issue directly and confronting the individuals who were causing the issue, they took what seemed like an easier way out and created blanket rules and applied them to everyone."
Julie: "Exactly! I'm not sure why I work here. I want to work for Toms, or someone with a purpose. I'm not sure what our purpose is here – to make a couple of extra bucks for our owner?"
Brian: "Are you looking for a new job?"
Julie: "Yes. I want to work somewhere that I can have an impact and make a difference. It likely means I'll take a pay cut, but I'm OK with that if it means I get do something more meaningful."

That's a real conversation with a real person, and I think you'll see that there's a lot going on in it. Julie's situation touches on purpose, empowerment and flexibility. I won't tell you what she ended up doing, but I will tell you that there are a lot of "Julies" out there – maybe one or two working for you, and wondering/considering whether to continue to do that.

Tips for Engaging Millennials

Now you might be thinking: "OK Brian, I get it. Millennials are different – and important – but what exactly do we do about that?" Here are some of the things we do at Olympus Group, at least partly with our Millennials in mind.

1. **Avoid Dumb Rules – and by the way, your employees can tell you if you have any.** Don't be afraid to ask your team members if they think you have dumb rules. No one wants dumb rules to control their actions or behaviors. One of the best ways to dis-engage a Millennial is to use phrases like *that's the way we do it around here,* or *that's how it's always been done,* or *in my day, nobody let me get away with that sort of thing.*

   Think about the previous example with Julie, and the rigid policy on starting time and finishing time. She viewed this as a "dumb rule." If her company was aware of that, and demonstrated more flexibility, it would probably help to improve retention.

2. **Practice Meritocracy: Reward performance over seniority**. As I've noted, Millennials can be impatient. So can everyone else. But the Millennials have demonstrated that they aren't afraid to change jobs when they feel they're being held back by a lesser performer, no matter how long that person may have been around.

   At Olympus, we believe we're a team, not a family. We reward top performers and replace mediocre performers, and we treat people fairly, not equally. I believe this resonates especially with our Millennials who can be impatient, but understand and place value in results.

3. **Benefits: Understand what your employees' value**. Make it a point to ask your team members what benefits they value. Ask them if there are any benefits they *wish* you offered. Don't forget to ask the same questions about perks, which are different than formal benefits. With the Millennials, the prevailing wisdom is to focus on flexibility and freedom as opposed to 401K's and fancy titles, but it's better to ask your team members what they value individually than to simply assume.

4. **Don't Skimp on the Praise.** Having grown up in a society of instant gratification, Millennials are used to receiving feedback just as fast. Quick example: When I took the CPA Exam twenty years ago, I had to wait almost two months for the results. Today, the results are instantaneous. Any Millennial who takes the exam knows immediately how they did. So, If someone is doing a good job, tell

them *exactly* that, and sooner rather than later. Positive reinforcements – "atta boys" and "atta girls" – go a long way.

5.   **Deliver regular feedback**. The traditional annual performance review does not work well with Millennials. The cycle is way too long. Millennials tend to want constant feedback as to whether they're meeting expectations. (It's also very important to ensure you have clearly set expectations in the first place!) We hold regular check in meetings, often weekly 1-1s, and it's particularly important to be honest with your Millennials, especially if they're not performing well.

6.   **Offer unique training opportunities**. Millennials tend to have a strong desire for personal growth and development. At Olympus Group, we've addressed this partly by offering "non-traditional" training opportunities, including mentorships and job shadowing.

7.   **Stop Calling them Millennials**. Millennials truly value their individuality and don't like to be stereotyped. (And that's probably true of everyone else on your team!)

I am by no means an expert on an entire generation. I do, however, believe if you put these tips into practice, you'll have a better chance of a more engaged group of Millennials working for you. And here's something else to consider. Millennials very often share their experiences online. They share their job experiences on Glassdoor, which is a website where current and former employees anonymously review companies. (Glassdoor also allows users to anonymously submit and view salaries as well as search and apply for jobs on its platform.) Millennials also talk about their employers on other social media. If you succeed at providing a great working environment for your Millennials, that could open the floodgates for other *motivated and engaged* younger people to want to join your team. Lots of benefits to creating a desirable place to work, right?

Across The Board

Now, on to increasing engagement across the board – regardless of generation or gender, blue collar or white collar, or any other differentiating factor. Let's focus on a common factor. *Everyone likes to feel appreciated.*

Think about children, continually looking for their parents' approval. After building a block tower, trying a new food or even just coloring inside the lines of a picture, off they go running to Mom or Dad seeking positive feedback.

Think about students, sitting in a classroom, eagerly raising their hands to be called on by the teacher. Why do they do that? They don't always get extra credit or a better grade because of it, but they do raise their hands so they can demonstrate their knowledge, and be told "good job" by the teacher. They want to be shown appreciation and get that pat on the back.

I even find myself looking for my wife Cindy's appreciation. "Honey. I just took out the trash" or "I did a load of laundry" – which usually leads to a well-deserved, sarcastic "I'm proud of you" or "about time" response.

Even the world's greatest professional athletes seek appreciation, and they perform better when they receive it. Think about "home-field advantage" for just a second. The home team tends to win more often than the visitor in every major sport. The playing field is the same size, the hoops are the same height, the balls or pucks are exactly the same, yet home teams win more often. (OK, baseball fields are not exactly the same, but they're all similar. Yet the home-field advantage still applies.)

Fivethirtyeight.com recently reported these home-field advantage percentages for the four major US sports leagues:

- NBA – 59.9% of the time the home team won
- NFL – 57.1% of the time the home team won
- NHL – 55.1% of the time the home team won
- MLB – 54% of the time the home team won

There are certainly other factors at play in home-field advantage – if nothing else, players getting a better night's sleep the night before the game, in their own beds! But *appreciation* is a factor. After a big dunk by the home team in a basketball game, the crowd goes wild and that creates *momentum*. The players' adrenaline rushes, and they find that extra gear. This is a direct result of the crowds' cheers – which represent the appreciation they are feeling for their home team's play.

Employees are no different. They want and seek appreciation, and one of the keys to increasing engagement levels in the workplace is simply to *show* that appreciation. An occasional pat on the back goes a long way toward accomplishing that, but here are what I think are some shocking statistics, which indicate that it's just not happening.

According to OC Tanner research (a consulting firm focused on employee recognition):

- 79% of employees who quit their jobs state that lack of appreciation was a major reason for leaving
- 65% of American workers state they weren't recognized even once last year for their performance
- 82% of employees feel that their supervisor does not recognize them for what they do
- 60% say they are more motivated by recognition than by money

This doesn't seem like rocket science. If managers give their employees the recognition they've earned, showing genuine appreciation, then they will almost certainly drive significantly better results. Sharing appreciation will probably also lift the spirits of everyone involved, including themselves, creating a positive energy that becomes contagious and causes a ripple effect across the entire organization. Much like a smile is contagious – more on smiling and employee engagement later on – positive feedback is both infectious and contagious.

By the way, don't discount what I just said about "including themselves." According to research by *Psychology Today*, *showing* gratitude can increase a person's wellness, improving sleep habits, increasing metabolism and decreasing stress. By *showing* appreciation, you're not only boosting employee performance and engagement, you're also improving your own health and well-being!

And the best part about all of this may be that showing this kind of appreciation doesn't have to cost a dime. All it takes is a little effort and focus. Just spend the time to notice and track your peoples' performance. Walk around and catch your employees doing something well, and then deliver that positive feedback – instantly! Just like the parent who praises their child for building the "biggest and best block tower in the world," or the coach who tells a player "great job" after an outstanding play. If you're willing to invest the time – and apply the focus – you'll probably find many opportunities each day to recognize individual employee accomplishments and deliver praise. Believe me, it's worth it – especially when you consider the (lack of any) cost!

****

Hey, it's Dave jumping in here. Brian wrote earlier about MBWA– Managing By Wandering Around. That's what he's talking about here, and I have my own MBWA story to tell. It goes back to the summer between my sophomore and junior years of college, when I worked on the maintenance crew at a manufacturing plant. We made heavy industrial fuses at the Chase Shawmut Company, and the process included metal stamping, tube cutting, wiring and all kinds of other operations, spread out over about 100,000 square feet of floor space.

I didn't do any of that technical stuff. I mowed the lawn, washed the windows, and yes, cleaned the toilets. But for about three weeks in the middle of the summer, I was also the sweeper. Every other day, I started sweeping in the northwest corner of the shop floor. I was expected to sweep half of the floor that day, in addition to my other chores. The next day, I picked up where I left off, and swept my way to the southeast corner.

I probably had 50 conversations each day with my fellow employees as I swept around their workstations. Nothing remarkable, just "how are you today?" and "what's Billy up to?" – this was a small town, and I knew lots of my fellow employees' brothers and sisters and cousins and kids, from school, sports, etc. I quickly noticed that there was someone else having lots of conversations with the same people each day, the shop foreman, who was probably the scariest-looking person I'd ever met to that point in my life. He was big, with huge arms and a perpetual scowl, and a fat half-smoked cigar in the middle of it most of the time.

I eventually learned that the scowl was just his face, not

his heart. More often than not, it seemed, his MBWA conversations ended with a literal pat on the back, or a thumbs-up as he walked away. Though you wouldn't think it to see his face, he ran a happy shop. And a productive shop.

People told me that he could be every bit as scary as he looked. "You don't want to be on his bad side," I was told. But I was also told: "You don't want to let him down." Even as a college-age kid, I understood the difference between those two feelings. People didn't want to let him down because they respected him, not just because there was some reason to fear him.

There was one particular day when he came to one particular station while I was sweeping around it. All of a sudden, there he was behind me, with his hand on my shirt collar, asking the operator at that station: "Is this college boy bothering you?" The operator said no, with a smile, and then said: "You know, he's not the worst sweeper we ever had."

The foreman said: "That's what I've been hearing. He does a pretty good job on the toilets too." Then his hand went from my collar to my back, and delivered a light pat. "You're a good kid," he said, "we like having you here."

I don't want to say that this was the worst job I ever had. In fact, the previous summer, I'd worked at the same plant as a degreaser, running metal fuse parts through various chemical washes to remove all the grease from the cutting and stamping processes. *That* was the worst job I ever had. But still, this job was menial and repetitive and boring.

But I was good at it. The foreman said so. He said he valued my contribution, that *the company* valued my contribution. So I continued to do good work at my menial job all summer long.

****

Dave's story certainly reinforces my point. But it also reminds me that we have to be consistent in this practice. I'm embarrassed to admit that we haven't always been. Not too long ago, one of our own employee engagement surveys indicated that we had at least a few team-members who didn't feel appreciated.

I don't want to be "do as I say, not as I do" guy. On the other hand, I/we are obviously not perfect at Olympus Group. So let me just say this. We try to learn from every mistake, and we try to react to every failure. In other words, when we learn we're not living up to our own expectations, we re-commit to the things we know to be important to our success.

Now, having got that off my chest, here are a few of the "appreciation things" we try to do consistently.

Hand-Written Notes

If you want to stand out in today's society of email, social media and cat memes, a handwritten note can do that. In the printing industry, we like to say that we put ink on paper, but we tend to do it in mass quantities. What I'm talking about here is the most personal application of "ink on paper" – just taking the time to write a few words of appreciation to someone who's important to you.

One of my favorite applications of this strategy is to write a note to a new employee on his or her first day, welcoming them to the team, explaining how excited I am that they are joining us, maybe even noting how impressed the whole hiring team was with their interview/resume. I think another pretty obvious application is to write a few sentences to an employee who's gone above and beyond, and just leaving it on their desk, or perhaps taped to their locker.

Maybe less obvious:

- A quick note to someone who never seems to miss a day of work
- A quick note to someone who always seems to have a positive attitude
- A quick note to someone who does something outside of work which reflects well on your company

How about prospects and customers, or even suppliers? If you want to stand out with a prospect, send a handwritten note after a call or a meeting. Don't just say *thank you for your time*, though. That only addresses part of the engagement opportunity. Did you learn something interesting or unique about the person or the company? Mention that! Maybe by writing something like: "*The thing that really stood out to me was...*" This is an opportunity to differentiate yourself, first with the handwritten note, and then by showing that you were paying attention!

With a customer, you'll never go wrong with a handwritten note thanking them for their business, but don't limit yourself to that. How about a note of congratulations for something they've accomplished, or a note of sympathy if that's what's called for. And with suppliers, you have the same sort of opportunity to deepen a relationship.

My advice is to buy some simple stationary and some stamps, then set aside maybe half an hour each week to "Write Thank You's" – and then write away. Why half an hour? Assuming that each note takes, say, three minutes, that's enough time for 10 notes each week. If this advice *forces you* to come up with 10 people to write to, that will be 10 positive engagements that might not have happened otherwise.

A hand-written note is an easy – and inexpensive! – way to stand out in a busy, cluttered world. Sure, you could send a text, or fire off an email, but look back at three words I used earlier – *above and beyond*. That's what *handwritten* does for you.

Celebrating Promotions

Here's an all-too-common missed opportunity: An employee has just been promoted and most companies would simply send out an email like this:

> "Please help me congratulate Jane Doe on her promotion to Vice-President. Jane has been a key factor in our success over the past 5 years."

What a missed opportunity! You promoted someone – probably because they did a great job! – and you publicly recognized it with an email. That's good as far as it goes, but take it a step further, send out the email but then do *more* to recognize the promotion.

You could have new business cards, with the new title, printed and ready to go before the promotion. You could make an announcement over the PA system. You could write the whole story up in your newsletter, explaining *why* this individual was promoted. You could post a photo in your lunchroom. There are any number of things that you could do, right? Here's the important part. These are all things that would add to the experience for the person being promoted, but they are also things that would highlight this individual's success so others can emulate it! And none of these things is particularly expensive, so you get two for the (pretty modest) price of one!

At Olympus, we're willing to spend a little more. We keep a case of champagne on hand, and for every promotion, I personally present a bottle of champagne (or sparkling grape juice if that's more appropriate) to recognize the accomplishment. We don't open it at work, but maybe not for the reason you think. What we really want is for the employee to take the bottle home and pop it open to celebrate with friends and/or family. See, on one level, the bottle of champagne is one way we can say *we value you*. When they take it home, though, it's a tangible piece of evidence that says *they value me – they* being *the people I work for*.

Again, two for the price of one. A simple, inexpensive gesture, but also another way to demonstrate appreciation. And for what it's worth, I think a bottle of champagne has more meaning than something like a gift card in a situation like this. I could be wrong. What do you think? In your company, you get to choose!

Pick Up The Phone

As noted, email and texting tend to be the primary methods of communication today. So you've started writing hand-written notes. Want another way to stand out? Pick up the phone! Yes, it's kind of crazy to think that, today, you can stand out by picking up the phone and making a call. That's the world we live in.

I travel a lot, and I spend a lot of time driving in my own car and rental cars. To maximize this driving time, I try to have a call list queued up and ready. (These are hands-free, Bluetooth-connection calls, by the way. I need to include that in case my mom ever reads this book.) I try not to get into anything too heavy while I'm driving, but I've found that it's the perfect time to give our superstars a call, and some of our customers, just to "check in" and to say thanks.

Awards

Recognizing employees for their years of service is a pretty common practice. In some companies, after 5 years, you get a clock with your company's logo on it, and after 25 years you get a really nice watch. I'm not opposed to recognizing years of service, in fact, we do it at Olympus and it is a nice way to pat your long-term employees on the back.

I think there's an opportunity to take these "annual awards" a step further, though, much like the professional sports leagues who hand out all sorts of hardware/awards: MVP (most valuable player), Rookie of the Year, Defensive Player of the Year, Comeback Player of the Year, Cy Young, Heisman Trophy, etc. These awards are given to top performers, and I believe that every company should do the same thing. At Olympus, we look for any excuse to publicly recognize our top employees. It may start with years of service, but we try to go well past that to recognize our superstars.

We give out a group of "Of The Year" awards every year. We start the process by asking for nominations in every category, and then I select and publicly recognize the winners at our holiday party. We give awards – which also include cash bonuses – for each of our core values (Most Selfless, Best "Can Do" Attitude, the Gets Results Award and the Integrity Award). This gives me an opportunity to emphasize the importance of our core values and tell stories tied to each one.

We want this to be fun, too, so we've made up other awards. Last year, we gave out awards for the Scrap Commander and the Quality Superstar. In the past, we've given the Gumby Award to recognize our most flexible employees who are willing to do anything. We've had the Go Getter Award, and we're very proud to name our own Rookie of the Year every year. All of this allows us to pat our superstars on the back, by publicly recognizing each winner.

Remember this statistic: "79% of employees who quit their jobs claim that a lack of appreciation was a major reason for leaving." I firmly believe that these awards and public accolades have helped us to retain some of our top talent over the years. Obviously, the bonus money is part of it too, but what we hear from our winners is that the recognition means at least as much.

Employee of the Month

Yes it's a little corny but don't overlook this simple way to recognize your top contributors. The best part of an employee of the month program is that, well, it happens every month! It's an annual-award-level recognition program that happens 12 times each year.

At Olympus, we solicit nominations every month, and we make a big deal of it. We strongly encourage our employees to nominate their co-workers. And then, we recognize not just the winner, but every nominee, and we share the reason(s) why they were nominated in our monthly newsletter. Do you see how this gives us the opportunity to pat a number of "additional" employees on the back every month? (We do the same thing with our annual awards, by the way.) Some months, we've had as many as 15 nominees! All of this allows us to reinforce the traits and behaviors that we value, and it's another example of something that doesn't cost a lot of money. Our Employee of the Month gets $100, but the money is a drop in the bucket, especially considering that it's a direct reward to one of our superstars. In my opinion – and my actual experience! – it's well worth it.

Measurement & Accountability

OK, you might be thinking, this is all great Brian, but not everyone on my team is going above and beyond and deserving of a pat on the back. In fact some of them aren't even deserving of a smile. How do I create high levels of engagement with people who aren't superstars?

I'm glad you asked. Two important steps are to measure their performance and hold them accountable – and that's true of superstars and poor performers alike. According to Gallup research: "Employees who strongly agree that their manager holds them accountable for their performance are 2.5 times more likely to be engaged in their job."

The fact of the matter is that most employees want feedback and are willing to be held accountable. To put that simply, they (1) want to do a good job, (2) want to know if they are, and (3), want to know how to improve if they are not. There's that old saying about how, *if it ain't broke, don't fix it.* Here's a related truth: *If you don't know that it's broke, you can't fix it!* It's not smart or fair to ask employees to fix performance problems they don't know that they have.

Measurement. Feedback. Accountability. When these come together in the right way, they are powerful motivators. But you have to be careful, especially with the first element of the process, because feedback and accountability based on bad measurement or metrics can be an even more powerful demotivator.

Put yourself in an employee's shoes. If you're being evaluated on metrics that (a) aren't clearly measurable, (b) that you don't agree with in the first place, or (c), that have no correlation to the company's overall success, you probably won't be highly motivated. So how do you know if your metrics are correct and positive?

My advice starts with this, don't measure too much stuff! It's easy to get carried away, and with today's Business Intelligence software and powerful data analytics, it can be tempting to measure everything that can possibly be measured. Don't do that! Ideally, focus on one meaningful number – the most meaningful number. That isn't to say you can't review other metrics, but think about the value of focusing on just one thing at a time. And then, when you "move the needle" on that particular metric, you can move on to the next most meaningful number.

It's also important to ensure that an individual employee can actually move *that* needle on *that* metric. If they can't significantly influence a metric personally, they won't be motivated by it.

Finally, it's important that the metrics your people are being measured on are part of your day-to-day conversations with them. You can't just bring this stuff up at an annual performance review. That won't influence daily behavior, and it won't provide day-to-day motivation.

We'll have more for you on measurement and accountability later on. For now, let me just say that, in all of my experience, everyone but the P3's – the *purposely poor performers* – will respond well to being measured against fair and meaningful metrics and held accountable for performance. Your superstars are by definition doing well, so this sort of management strategy provides you with another regular opportunity to pat them on the back. Your "room for improvement" employees are solid contributors, but not yet superstars. This is how you show them and motivate them to superstar level. Your "need to improve" employees may be your greatest opportunity. Ignore them and they won't improve. Scold them and they might improve.

Teach them and work with them – share the detail on current performance and how to get better – and they probably will improve.

As for the P3's, I believe in giving everyone at least one chance to turn things around. But I also believe that anyone who won't work for you, can't work for you – with *can't* being your choice, not theirs.

Smile More!

Just one more quick thought before I turn this back over to Dave. I wrote earlier that smiling is contagious. Here's a quick, easy tip to improve your life: *Smile more!*

"Smiling can be a competitive advantage – it makes every person feel a little better, and every situation a little brighter." – Richard Branson

Whether you're walking around the office, talking to co-workers, having dinner with your spouse or even when you're on the phone, try to smile more. Try smiling during an intense negotiation, it will often cut the tension and ease the mood.

Smiling is free and it really is contagious. It boosts your mood and the mood of those around you. Just give it a shot, try smiling a little more and see the impact it has on others around you! A simple, sincere smile will improve your level of engagement with whomever you are speaking with.

6 Into The Funnel
Dave Fellman

So, are you smiling right now? When Brian sent me the last chapter, the last section was followed by a note: *Does this belong here? Or even in the book?* My response: *Hell, yes!* I might not have said that *smiling* is contagious, but I know that *mood* is contagious, and a smile is an indication of mood, right? I have also observed that mood flows downhill in business – when the boss is in a bad mood, that tends to affect everyone. So I see two options, use your facial expression to push everyone's mood down or to pull it up.

OK, back to sales engagement. Earlier, I expressed my feeling that your website should be the entryway into your sales funnel, and possibly even your store. I posed three scenarios: First, your product or service can be easily purchased online, so your website is a full-fledged store. Second, your product or service can be purchased online, but options and/or other issues make that more complex. Third, your product or service can't be purchased online. It's just too customized and/or complex.

If you fit into the first scenario, any *suspect* who engages with your advertising and takes the next step – into the store! – probably qualifies as a *prospect*. Remember the three qualifying criteria:

1. They buy, want or need what you sell
2. They buy, want or need enough of it to make pursuing them worthwhile
3. They show some real interest in buying from you

In a retail situation, the fact that *they* take initiative to take that next step probably satisfies #1 and #3, and in retail, #2 is not as large a consideration. Yes, as I've noted, there is almost always a cost attached to acquiring a new customer. In fact, there is a cost attached to making every sale. But in retail, the cash component of the acquisition cost has already been spent. In other words, that was your advertising cost. When that advertising engagement brings someone into the store, you are reaping the return on that investment!

So what other cost/investment do you have to deal with? I'm sure you've heard the expression that *time is money*. Here's another fundamental concept: *You should never spend more time than you need to in any engagement, be it suspect, prospect, customer, employee or anyone else.*

The key words in that statement, of course, are *need to*. Let's go back to our discussion of *greeting* and *expression of appreciation*. You need to *greet* at the beginning of the engagement. You need to *express appreciation* at the end of the engagement. You need to *take care of business* in between. That can range from answering questions to taking an order to providing the product to collecting the money.

I'm hoping to make two points here. The first is that you should never take *less* time than you need to do all of this properly, but you should never take *more* time either! Time *is* money. And just like money, you can do one thing with it, or you can do another thing – but unless you have an unlimited supply of time or money, you can't do *everything*. What I'm really talking about here is *efficiency*.

Now tell me if this sounds familiar. You have a million things to do today, so you're guaranteed to get to the end of the day with some of those things left undone. Thinking back on the day so far, you've probably spent more time than you had to, or really wanted to, on several things already, all of which means that you get to the end of the day having done even less than you might have.

No tell me if *this* sounds familiar. One of those things that took longer than you really wanted it to was a buying engagement. You were the customer in this engagement, and it was *the seller* who made it take longer than you thought was really necessary. Maybe a greeting that went too far into something other than the business you came in to take care of today. Maybe a lack of knowledge or understanding during the taking care of business stage. Maybe the salesperson launching an attempt at a "social" conversation after the business transaction was complete.

Do you see how an "extra-long" engagement like that can be a negative for both parties? You're spending more time than you need to in order to get something done. Your counterpart is also spending more time than he or she needs to – and he/she probably has a full plate too, right? What I'm talking about now is *inefficiency*!

Please understand, I'm not talking about taking shortcuts here. I do want you to invest the time you *need to* for a successful engagement. And if you're going to err, I guess I want you to err on the side of too much rather than too little. But's let's try for only a little too much.

Maybe I can say it this way. Be respectful of *their* time. Be thrifty with *your* time. Because *time is money* for everyone.

Second Point

The second point I'm hoping to make is that all the same rules apply for a website engagement. *Greeting. TCB. Expression of Appreciation.* One of the questions I asked you to consider earlier was whether your website makes a good first impression? Another was whether it makes it clear how to take the next step? That's where the *greeting* transitions into *taking care of business*. Whether it's menu-driven or search-driven, your website must help your suspects, prospects, etc. get to where they need to go.

Take a look at Olympus Group's website: www.olympusgrp.com. Across the top of the home page, you'll see both menus and a search icon. You'll also see headlines and graphics which I think do a pretty good job of communicating what Olympus sells. The "top left" section of the home page focuses on the printing side of the business, and the "top right" on the mascot side. Both sections support the headlines and graphics with some explanatory text, but more importantly, both feature a "Learn More" button. *Are you interested? Here's how to take the next step!*

I also like the section immediately below these two, where OG starts to tell it's supporting story:

Olympus Group is a leader in bringing creative ideas to life.

Hence our motto: Imagine it. Done.

How do we do it? We have assembled the widest range of in-house large format digital printing capabilities in the US, so we have complete control over timelines, materials, and project execution. Olympus Group has helped brands known around the world with textile printing, indoor & outdoor signage, vehicle wraps, and more. We are also proud to be the go-to creator for beloved mascots of all types for teams and brands

Note the difference in font size. The relative size is not exactly the same in this book as it is on the web page, but I think it represents the purpose and intent.

Mission

Motto

Explanation

Now, I know it's not the actual mission statement, which is: *At Olympus, we want to create a rewarding work environment for our team.* But we could think of this as an "external" mission statement that reflects the benefit derived from Olympus' "internal" mission.

Think back to our conversation about features and benefits. *We have created a rewarding work environment for our team* would definitely qualify as a feature of Olympus Group. It isn't stated on the website, but it's there to be brought into play at the appropriate time. *We have assembled the widest range of in-house large format digital printing capabilities in the US* is another feature. And why is that important? Because it gives us *complete control over timelines, materials and project execution.*

You may or may not buy the printing for your business. If you do, the printing you buy may or may not be as complex as the sort of printing OG produces day in and day out. You may remember that Brian and I met at a conference run by the Specialty Graphics and Imaging Association – *Specialty* being the key word. The typical OG project has a lot of moving parts, and the typical Specialty Graphics buyer is *painfully* aware of that. You're familiar with Murphy's Law, right? *What can go wrong will go wrong.* I think it's fair to say that Murphy alone is bad enough, when you have subcontractors involved – in other words, when you're *not* just using your in-house capabilities – you're dealing with Murphy's whole family! *Complete control* is a significant benefit.

But I'm not trying to sell you on Olympus Group. I'm trying to sell you on effective engagement strategy, and reminding you that effective engagement is a process, not an event. The fundamental idea is for B to build on A, and C to build on A and B, and so on. A is the Mission Statement. B is the feature. C is the benefit. And D, in this case, takes us into the realm of "supporting evidence." *Olympus Group has helped brands known around the world with textile printing, indoor & outdoor signage, vehicle wraps, and more. We are also proud to be the go-to creator for beloved mascots of all types for teams and brands around the country.*

I'd like you also to consider that none of those elements would work as well all alone. "We're a leader…" *OK, everyone says stuff like that.* "Hence our motto…" *Hey, that's kind of cool.* "How do we do it…" *Oh, yeah, that's important to me. Maybe they really are leaders in bringing creative ideas to life!*

A plus B plus C and so on. And here's some more fundamental business wisdom: *It is never the buyer's responsibility to communicate with the seller. It is always the seller's responsibility to communicate with the buyer.* That actually means two things. One is that it's not your customers' responsibility to stay in touch with you. It's your responsibility to stay in touch with them. We'll talk more about that when we talk about Customer Maximization. The point for right now is that it's never their responsibility to *understand* what you're trying to communicate. It's your responsibility to make sure that the dots get connected, that real communication occurs. And please remember that my definition of selling is to *help them* to make the decision to buy from you.

Branding

Let's go back to that "supporting evidence" for just a moment. *Olympus Group has helped brands known around the world with textile printing, indoor and outdoor signage, vehicle wraps and more.* I promised to come back to the topic of *branding*, and this seems like a good time for it.

What is *branding* anyway? I found a list of 30 definitions at www.heidicohen.com. Ms. Cohen prefaced her list by noting that "*brands* have a wide range of uses for businesses, products and individuals in today's dynamic marketing landscape where publishing and message distribution are no longer limited to media entities." She also noted that a brand, by itself, is not a marketing strategy – and I would add that a brand, by itself, is not an *engagement* strategy. But it's all a part of the way you should be thinking about engaging with your suspects, prospects, customers and maximized customers.

Here are my four favorites from Ms. Cohen's list, along with attributions:

"A **brand** is the set of expectations, memories, stories and relationships that, taken together, account for a consumer's decision to choose one product or service over another. If the consumer (whether it's a business, a buyer, a voter or a donor) doesn't pay a premium, make a selection or spread the word, then no brand value exists for that consumer." *Seth Godin* – author of *This Is Marketing and 18 other books – and one of my personal heroes!*

"**Branding** is the representation of your organization as a personality. Branding is who you are that differentiates you." *Dave Kerpen* – author of *Likeable Social Media*

"**Branding** is what lazy and ineffective marketing people do to occupy their time and look busy." *David Meerman Scott* – author of *Real-Time Marketing and PR*

"**Brand** is the sum total of how someone perceives a particular organization. Branding is about shaping that perception." *Ashley Friedlein* – founder of *Econsultancy*

As Ashley Friedlein points out, *brand* and *branding* are two different things. Think about Miller High Life beer, a big name brand from Brian's hometown of Milwaukee. When you order a Miller, you know what you're getting. And going back a few years, the Miller brand was the foundation for the pretty-much-instantaneous acceptance of Miller Light. It was, quite simply, the light beer from Miller.

Now think about Crank Arm, which is brewed less than half a mile from my home in Raleigh NC. It's good beer, but it's not yet a "big name" brand. Miller is at a stage where they can *capitalize* on their brand – probably even more so because the full name of the company is now MillerCoors, reflecting the 2008 merger of Miller and Coors, another "big name" brand. Crank Arm, on the other hand, is in the *branding* stage. They're working to build their brand, and as Friedlein put it, to *shape the perception* of their product.

A quick aside. When I was in high school – and first getting interested in beer! – everyone I knew was either a Bud guy or a Schlitz guy. There were other brands available, of course, including Miller High Life, "regional" beers like and Schaefer and Narragansett, and imported beers like Heineken and Tuborg. But Budweiser and Schlitz – The Beer That Made Milwaukee Famous! – were the clear market leaders.

This was Newburyport, MA in the late 1960's. By the early 1970's, I was off to college at the University of New Hampshire, which was only about 30 miles away in Durham, NH, but light years away in terms of eye-opening experience. During my Junior year, three of my dorm-mates went on a Spring Break ski trip to Colorado, driving 2000 miles each way for the secondary purpose of bringing back as much Coors beer as they could carry. Some quick research suggests that they paid something like $10.00 per case. I think I remember being told that they spend another $10.00 on a big tub and 2000 miles worth of ice. I distinctly remember buying two bottles from that stockpile, for $2 each – more than the price of a whole six-pack of Pabst Blue Ribbon, another Milwaukee beer, which was the go-to for budget-conscious students like myself back in those days.

So why would a budget-conscious college student pony up more than 6X the "normal" price for a bottle of beer? Because Coors' *branding* made me do it! It was *cold brewed*, don't you see, and they only sold it in Colorado and a few nearby states, because it had to stay cold, or else it lost its amazing taste. And sure, there was a supply-and-demand element to this opportunity – but that's the thing, it was an *opportunity* to experience a product I'd heard about (*branding*) which had special qualities (*branding*) and I really, really wanted to give it a try!

It's worth considering, I think, that my dorm-mates made the sale, but it was Coors that *engaged* me. In the introduction, I wrote that *engagement* means customers who *want to* buy from us, in addition employees who *want to* work for us, and even suppliers who really want to work *with* us. The Coors legend/branding accomplished that with me back in the 1970's.

For what it's worth, I don't drink as much beer as I used to. My wife teases me about having become a gin-snob and a wine-snob. Every once in a while, though, a nice cold beer seems like just the thing. And I'm still happy enough to order a Coors if it's on the menu. But if I'm around Raleigh, it's more likely to be a Crank Arm!

One more thought on branding. *Olympus Group is a leader in bringing creative ideas to life*. I referred to that as an "external" mission statement. It's probably more correct to call it a *branding statement*, and I'm sure Brian would tell you that those few words perfectly define the perception he's hoping to build.

Contact Capture

Going back to the functionality of the Olympus Group website, below the "story" section is more information about specific elements of the product line – and again, each one has a "Learn More" button. Below that is the section where OG captures the information it needs to follow up – name, email address, phone number and a "Tell Us More" box. You might notice that they're not trying to capture all of the "5 Why's and How" information here. In fact, the only *required* information is a name and email address.

Obviously, I would like to collect more data, but let's not forget that this is a *process*. If I have your name and your email address, I can probably identify your company with no more than one additional step. For example, if I left my own name and email address here – Dave Fellman, dmf@davefellman.com – it's pretty likely that my full name is David Something-That-Starts-With-An-M Fellman. (Marshall, if you're interested.) It's also pretty likely that you'll find more information at www.davefellman.com – www.whatever-comes-after-the @. So this "minimalist" approach still satisfies the requirement of capturing enough information to take the next step, and that creates the opportunity to fill in the rest of the blanks. Please note that this section of the website also invites a phone call, which creates the same opportunity to fill in all the blanks, especially the *what, why* and *when*.

By the way, I'd like to invite you to visit – and critique – my website: www.davefellman.com. Does it make a good first impression? Does it make it clear what I sell? Does it make it clear and easy how to take the next step?

The Best Part

Now we come to what I think is the best part of the Olympus Group website, the "Video & Media Watch Us On The Go" section at the bottom. Right on the main page, you'll find 7 short demo videos, and if you click on *Watch, Learn, Explore*, you find those again on a new page plus 11 more. It's been said that a picture is worth 1000 words. How many words is a "moving picture" worth – especially one with a voice track!

Let me back off on that statement, though. The videos themselves may not be the "best part" of what I think is a well-designed and highly functional website. But they are definitely the part that takes it to the next level. Words and images. Static *plus* dynamic. There are websites you can visit, and there are websites you can *engage* with – although that doesn't fully capture what I'm trying to say here.

Let's try again. There are websites that just sort of sit there when you visit, and then there are those that actively engage *you*. Where do you want *your website* to fall along that spectrum?

Third Degree

The more I think about it, the more I like the "minimalist" approach that Olympus Group's website takes to collecting follow-up information. As noted, an email address gives you the *where* for your follow-up plus a likely direction for further research. And, as noted, you will probably have the opportunity to fill in the blanks as you work through the process.

Here's some advice, though. Don't be in a massive, single-minded hurry to fill in those blanks. This takes us into an area that's a huge pet peeve of mine. Just yesterday, I called a company to inquire about a particular service, and the salesperson started the conversation by demanding my name, rank and serial number. Yes, I'm exaggerating – somewhat – but the tone of the conversation was still: *"I'm not going to help you until you help me."*

While I'm on this topic, let me rant on another pet peeve. My next call yesterday was an attempt at a selling engagement, not a buying engagement. In other words, I was calling one of my own suspects to see if I could sell her on my services. The receptionist asked for my name, and then asked me: "Will she know what this is about?"

I answered: "I think so." That may have been an exaggeration, but it felt justified because I had, in fact, sent an introductory email which promised a follow-up call. Had she read and remembered that email? I can't be sure.

But that's not the point anyway. Setting aside the fact that *what I sell* might be of real value to this company, what if I had been a potential customer – someone who's revenue potential might be of even greater and more immediate value? If you were the owner of this company, is that the way you would want me to be greeted?

Yes, you're busy. We just talked about that. And there are plenty of salesjerks who would absolutely waste your time. But there's another old saying about throwing babies out with bathwater – in this application, losing a good thing through your efforts to protect yourself from a bad thing. The mechanism for preventing that at the greeting stage via telephone is simply to screen all of your calls. And you may be thinking, well, isn't that what this receptionist was doing?

Please consider this. You can screen *actively* or *passively*. *Passively* means simply to take a message, and voice mail technology makes that easy and direct, right? *"She's not available right now. Can I put you through to her voice mail?"* It's not what the caller is hoping for, probably, but it's pretty well accepted as the means of modern business communication.

Actively means to challenge the caller, and while *"Will she know what this is about?"* is pretty benign along the range of possible challenges, my position is that it's an unnecessary question which may undermine the whole objective of the greeting stage. Let the caller leave a message. *Invite* the caller to leave a message. Then listen to the message to see if it's something you want to engage with. Why even take the chance of creating a less-than-ideal situation?

Am I especially sensitive to this? Maybe. But I'm pretty sure I'm not the only person who might feel less like buying from you if you make me feel less than fully welcome in your store. And remember, we've established an expanded definition of *store* which includes an office or even a call center.

Out To Lunch
As I'm writing this, I'm reminded of another day, maybe a month ago, when absolutely no one I wanted to talk to was available to talk to me. I was pretty frustrated by the end of that day, but probably not for the reason you

think. It wasn't because I ended up leaving voice mail messages for most of those people, and only one of them returned my call. It was because most of the people who answered the phone made the people I wanted to talk to look bad.

Throughout the morning, I heard several variations of: "He hasn't made it in yet." During the mid-day, I heard several variations of: "He (or she) is out to lunch." From about 3:00 PM on, I heard several variations of: "She's gone for the day."

Now, granted, these were mostly situations where I was calling as a seller, but again, what if I was calling as a potential buyer? Does "He hasn't made it in yet" inspire confidence in the person or the company? In the same vein, does "She's gone for the day" make you more or less likely to want to buy from them? And while everyone is entitled to be "out to lunch" for at least a part of every day, does a potential customer or anyone else need to know that?

I challenged you earlier to rate yourself and your team on how well you execute the greeting stage. If you didn't do it then, I hope you'll do it now. It's not just about being nice, it's also about making a *professional* first impression, and little things can make big differences!

Following Up

Let's go back to the three product-complexity scenarios I presented earlier. The first is that your product or service can be easily purchased online, so your website is a full-fledged store. If that's the case, let's assume that your website made the sale. You have either created a customer (in the case of a first time order), or taken a step toward customer maximization (a repeat order). Either way, there's a "next level" to be gained through further engagement, and we'll talk more about that when we get to the chapter on Customer Maximization.

The second scenario is that your product or service can be purchased online, but options and/or other issues make that more complex. As I wrote earlier, the ratio between *store* and *funnel entry* is probably 20/80 in this scenario, so maybe 80% of the time, this is where a salesperson has to pick up the ball. But here's a question, is it a close-the-sale salesperson, or a help-me-choose-the-best-option salesperson? Obviously, one salesperson can be

Into The Funnel **89**

both things, but not all salespeople have both skillsets and/or the requisite attitudes. And, as I mentioned earlier, not all salespeople even think of themselves as salespeople.

Let's stop here, then, and agree on a set of definitions. First, by my definition, s*elling* is *the act of helping suspects, prospects and customers to make the decision to buy from you.* Therefore, anyone who is doing any of those things is a *salesperson* – at least during any engagement during which they are doing what we just defined as *selling*.

The most important thing about following up on a "second scenario" website engagement is speed. I think anyone who (a) visits your website, and (b) chooses your "I need help" option should be considered a hot lead. So that means (1) there needs to be a clear "I need help" option, and (2) it has to be monitored. You must have a mechanism by which someone is alerted to every opportunity for follow-up.

Old Trick

This brings to mind an old trick from the Yellow Pages days. Let's say you were investing in a full-page ad in the Yellow Pages, and you wanted to be able to track the performance of that ad. On one hand, you could ask every caller how they happened to be calling, but that can be cumbersome – and also inappropriate for any call that wasn't about buying something from you. So what some companies did was get a special phone number for the Yellow Pages ad – a number that was only published in that ad – so any time that number rang, it had to have come from the ad.

On one hand, that made it easy to count the calls that came in as a result of the ad. Some companies took it to another level, though. In fact, I once worked for a company where the Director of Marketing (me!), went around to all of the telephones in the office and painted the button for the special line lime green. (You may have to be of a certain age to understand that. In the "old" days, we had console phones with buttons along the top or along the side for each line that could be accessed from that phone, and counting "inside" lines, 4-6 buttons was pretty common. When a line was ringing, a light under the button would blink. You pushed down on the button to connect the call to your phone. So any time anyone saw a green light blinking, they knew it was a "hot lead" from our Yellow Pages ad.)

It's also worth noting that I established a "hierarchy" for answering that line. We had a general rule that someone had to answer every phone call before the fifth ring. (This was pre-voice mail. No automated system picked up after X number of rings. The phone just kept on ringing until the caller gave up!) If you heard a phone ringing and saw a light blinking, you started counting, and if someone hadn't answered after the fourth ring, you did, regardless of what your position might be.)

The rule for the "green line" was that an inside salesperson (we had three of those) was to answer before the third ring. If that didn't happen, the receptionist was to answer before the fourth ring. If that didn't happen, we reverted to the rule that someone/anyone would answer before the fifth ring. The idea was to get what we knew were *sales inquiries* directly to a *sales*person — or perhaps I should say a *trained* salesperson, keeping in mind our established definition.

Modern Telephony

If I were faced with the same challenge today, I might still make use of a special number, or else I might use the menu function of a modern telephone system. *"If you know your party's extension, you may dial it at any time. If you're calling from our website to request personal assistance, please dial 1."* Again, this line must be monitored to ensure that you're able to continue the engagement.

That doesn't mean, by the way, that someone is always available to answer every call. An immediate connection is the best case scenario, of course, but in the modern world, I think it's fair to say that most of us would be happy with a "prompt" response. That will have different meaning to every individual, but I can tell you that, in my own case, I'm pretty happy if I get a return phone call from a "buying" inquiry within 10-15 minutes.

So we now have two possibilities. someone calls from your website and gets you right on the line, or someone calls from your website, leaves a message, and you call them back. Either way, we still have the basics of *Greeting, TCB,* and *Expression of Appreciation.*

Here's what I recommend for the *greeting* when answering the phone: "Hi, this is (your name), how can I help you today?"

Here's what I recommend for the *greeting* when returning a phone call: "Hi this is (your name) from (your company). I'm returning your call. How can I help you today?"

Hopefully, you're remembering the story about my visit to Ace Hardware. Not "Can I help you?" but "*How* can I help you!" Beyond that, the only fundamental difference between the two scenarios is to identify your company, and remind them that you're returning their call.

Casual or Professional?

There is one more thing I would like you to consider, though. Should you be (First name) or (First name + Last name)? On one hand, we are a casual society. First name alone is probably OK. But on the other hand, this is a professional engagement. If you believe, as I do, that First name + Last name might be perceived as a little bit more professional in a sales engagement, then adding your last name is a good strategy.

A quick aside. I have a client who buys in on the *professionalism* element, but has reason to be concerned with the privacy and safety of his employees. One of his inside salespeople was stalked by a customer a couple of years ago. The stalker looked up the salesperson on LinkedIn and Facebook, and attempted to connect on both platforms. He then started showing up at places that the salesperson was planning to be. Fortunately, the problem was resolved without issue, but it shook up the salesperson and her teammates. So the compromise we came up with was to have everyone use the name "Chris Kelly" when answering or returning website inquiry phone calls.

Unexpected Benefit

That actually turned out to provide an unexpected benefit. "Lots of our return calls ended up with us leaving messages for them," one of the inside salespeople told me. "But since we were all 'Chris Kelly', we didn't have to extend the phone tag. The chances were good that at least one of the 'Chris Kelly's' would be able to take the call when they called back." My client even established a "Chris Kelly of the Month" award to acknowledge the top performer in the inside sales department. (Brian loves that!)

Here's something else to consider, though. If you are returning a website inquiry call, and your party is not available, should you even ask them to call you back? The real question is this: Should you put the ball in their court – requiring them to take another step toward connecting with you – or keep it in yours?

Here's what I might recommend. If you find yourself in *their* voice mail on your first attempt, say something like this: "Hi this is (your name) from (your company). I'm returning your call. But rather than ask you to call me back, I'm going to try you again in XX minutes. If we don't connect then, I'll ask you to call me at your convenience."

What's the thinking behind this recommendation? First and foremost, remember what I said about *responsibility* and *communication*. It is *never* the buyer's responsibility to communicate with the seller. It is *always* the seller's responsibility to communicate with the buyer. And it is *always* to the seller's advantage to make communication as easy as possible for the buyer.

Beyond that, a prompt return call communicates an important impression: *I value your business!* Beyond even that, the voice mail situation provides you with an opportunity to make a promise, and then keep it. *"I will try you again in XX minutes."* When you keep that promise, you add something else to your positioning: *When I say something is going to happen, you can take it to the bank!*

So on one hand, you can say "Tag, you're it!" On the other hand, you can use this situation to build a foundation for a more successful engagement. Which seems like better strategy? Just remember, if you *don't* keep your promise, you are undermining that foundation.

Then, if you don't connect on the second attempt, here's what you might say: "Hi this is (your name) from (your company). As promised, I'm trying again to return your call. Since we didn't connect, I think it's probably best for me to ask you to call me at your convenience. The number is…"

Third Scenario

OK, let's go back again to the three product-complexity scenarios I presented earlier. The third scenario was that your product or service can't be purchased online because it's just too customized and/or complex. In this scenario, we're far more likely to be talking about *commercial* vs. *retail* – although let's not forget that commercial is not limited to B2B. There are plenty of examples of complex products and/or services that are purchased by non-business consumers.

Let's also go back to the purpose of commercial advertising – *to get people into the funnel, where a salesperson can engage, qualify and hopefully succeed at turning suspects into customers.*

Everything I wrote earlier about the second scenario still applies. This is an opportunity to (1) engage, (1a) qualify, and (2) hopefully succeed at turning this suspect into a customer. Just remember that we're still talking about a *suspect!* The fact that *they* initiated the contact is certainly an indication of interest, but it can still be a long way from a commitment to buy. And also, please remember that nobody needs a drill bit, they need a hole!

Tell Me About...

So let's say that I initiate a "third scenario" inquiry with you, and you ask me, "How can I help you today?"

I answer: "I'd like to get more information about (what you sell)."

I hope you won't immediately tell me everything there is to know about your product or service. Instead, I hope you will *ask* me about *my application* for your product or service.

Let's rewind the tape to see how we got here in the first place. You advertised. I responded. I visited your website, where I found all kinds of information about your product or service, but I still took the "call or click" option because what I know already (from your ad, from your website, from anywhere/everywhere else I might have explored before calling or clicking) hasn't provided me with all the knowledge I need to make a buying decision.

Knowledge is the key word here. My current state of inquiry is probably somewhere along a scale from "I don't know if your product in general is the right tool for my job" to "I don't know which of your products – what model or options – is the right tool for my job" to "Is your version of the right tool for my job a better choice than a competitor's version?"

Do you see how this all hinges around the application? So that's what you talk about!

This is the essence of *consultative* selling. *Tell me what you're hoping to accomplish. I'll share my expertise to help you identify the right tool for the job.* To put that in different terms, *let me help you to make the decision about what to – or even whether to – buy from me!*

7 Qualified Prospects
Dave Fellman

So far, most of what I've written applies mainly to *suspect engagement*. Remember, they are *suspects* when you have reason to think (or even hope) they might be prospects. They are prospects only when you know that they're fully *qualified*, and that means you *know* – not just think or hope! – that they buy, want or need (1) exactly what you sell, (2) enough of it to make pursuing them worthwhile, and (3) they have some real interest in buying from you. That leads to some more fundamental wisdom. It's really pretty easy to sell to a fully qualified prospect. But it's nearly impossible – and a poor use of time! – to sell to anyone who fails two or more of the qualifying criteria.

What all of that means is that your first stage of follow-up must be about qualifying. That's what the "tell me about…" conversation is really all about. What's interesting is that this sort of *consultative* strategy also stands to position you as an expert, not just a salesperson.

Is that important? Let me ask you this, when you think *salesperson*, does that call to mind a flattering image? As I wrote earlier, *selling* means different things to different people. Some of us think of it as an honorable profession. Others – many others! – equate salespeople with slithering reptiles, and I think it's fair to say that some of that is justified.

I remember a salesperson who described his qualifying process to me this way: "I'm gonna sell you something. I just don't know what yet!" Thinking back on that statement, I suppose that he might have been talking about doing a needs analysis to determine which of his products was the right tool for my job. But that's not the way I perceived it. I think he was more of that hard-chargin', deal-makin', close-or-die kind of salesperson. He was also, I learned later, an underachiever, struggling to make a living as a salesperson and not making his employers very happy either.

Four Possibilities

As I stated earlier, engagement is a process, not an event. Making a sale is a very specific type of engagement process. Sometimes it's a short process. Other times, it lasts much longer. And in fact, there's another important set of variables. Sometimes it's an easy process, and sometimes it's very, very hard.

Those two sets of variables give us four possibilities:

1. Short and Easy
2. Short and Hard
3. Long and Easy
4. Long and Hard

Short and Easy is often the result of a successful suspect engagement:

- I'd like to get more information, followed by…
- Tell me about your application, followed by…
- Based on what you've told me, here's what I think would work best…
- …followed by YES!

Short and Hard, in my experience, is often related to a price objection. I'll have more to say about dealing with those in just a moment.

Long and Easy is generally related to timing more than anything else. Some people just take a long time to get to yes. We might call them careful buyers. Sometimes other factors – like cash flow – stretch the process. *I want this. I'm going to buy this. I'm going to buy this from you. I just don't have the money right now.* It's important to note that a "hard sell" strategy is usually the worst way to approach either a careful buyer or a cash flow situation. Patience is very often a virtue!

Long and Hard generally reflects a complex sale with any number of issues, obstacles and/or objections, including price. Obviously, *long and hard* requires the most follow-up – and usually the most creative follow-up.

That takes us to the topic of *persistence*, which is generally considered to be a positive attribute for a salesperson. Unfortunately, too much of what I see is what I call *blind* persistence – calling and calling and emailing and calling without adding anything of value to the relationship. That's not *engagement*, is it? More on that to follow.

Price Objections

As noted, the *short and hard* scenario is often related to a price objection.

- I'd like to get more information, followed by…
- Tell me about your application, followed by…
- Based on what you've told me, here's what I think would work best, followed by…
- *That's more than I want to spend!*

Now, I could have expressed the last part of that differently, perhaps ranging from *"I think you're trying to take advantage of me"* to *"I see the value in your proposition, but it's just more than I can afford."* I chose my words carefully, though, because I think they represent the essence of *all* price objections, with *want to* as the key words.

Here's an observation. *No one wants to spend more than they have to for anything.* That includes you and me, right? But here's another observation. In my experience, *most people will spend what they have to in order to get what they want or need* – subject only to the caveat of being able to afford it. Do you see that the key words now are *have to*?

The best way to be able to overcome a price objection is to be able to say: *This is how much you'll have to spend in order to get what you've told me that you want or need.*

Needs and Wants

The first stage of the "tell me about…" conversation is often called *needs* analysis, but in fact, it should encompass both *wants* and *needs*. The *needs* part is pretty straightforward, encompassing whatever is needed in order to fulfill the purpose of the purchase.

That takes us back to the drill bit and the hole. The drill bit was the means to the end, the tool required to meet my ultimate need. And remember, the "specifications" of the hole determined exactly which drill bit I needed.

Where do *wants* fit in? Setting aside the fact that I didn't know exactly what I needed when I walked into the store, I could probably have saved myself some money by leaving Ace Hardware without buying, and ordering the same drill bit on Amazon. That might have saved me money, but cost me time.

So, did I *need* to complete my project that day? Not really. But I *wanted* to, and that had some value for me.

Let's extend that to something that happens frequently in Brian's business. As I noted earlier, a typical Olympus Group project has a lot of moving parts, and timing is one of them. *When do you need this* is always part of the conversation, and the answer tends to be *sooner* rather than *later*. But experience has shown that the question being answered is not always the question being asked.

For example, Customer A might say: "I need it by Friday, because I'm getting on a plane Saturday morning, heading out to a trade show, and this graphic is a critical part of our exhibit." Customer B might say: "I need it by Friday, even though I don't leave for the trade show until next Tuesday, but I don't want to have to worry about this particular graphic over the weekend." Those aren't the same levels of *need*, are they? In fact, I think the second scenario fully qualifies as a *want*. "I don't *need* it until next Tuesday, but I *want* it done before that." Fundamentally, it doesn't even matter why. Both *needs* and *wants* are real things, even if they do rate a different level of criticality.

We Have A Situation!

Now, let's complicate the situation even further. Let's make both Customer A's *need* and Customer B's *want* due the same Friday! And let's also say that there aren't enough standard resources available to complete both orders by Friday – all the people, presses, etc. have already been fully scheduled.

Resources can be added, however. Putting myself into Brian's shoes, I could ask one of my production teams to work overtime on Thursday. So I engage with those team members, and they agree to work the extra hours, in fact, they're probably happy to earn some time-and-a-half!

But because of that time-and-a-half, I now have to quote at least one of these customers a higher-than-normal price in order to preserve my profitability. Should it be Customer A, Customer B, or both?

My personal opinion is that it should be Customer B, but that's based on an assumption – the assumption that Customer A was the first to "reserve" these resources. Maybe I should just say that, whichever order was accepted first, knowing the timeline, the *other* order is the one which requires the additional resources.

So now I'm going to have to tell Customer B that we can commit to the Friday delivery, but in order to do that, there will have to be overtime and it will have to be included in the price. The customer says: "How much?" I tell him. The customer says: "Is there any way to avoid that?" I say: "Yes. If you can give us until end-of-day Monday, we can get the job done without any overtime."

What would you say to that if you were Customer B? I can definitely picture him now saying: "Sure, I can live with that." It didn't satisfy his (or her) *want*, perhaps, to not have to worry about the graphic over the weekend, but it did meet the *need*. And here's a fundamental truth. If you want happy customers, you have to meet *all* of their needs, but only *most* of their wants. And, of course, you have to know the difference.

Rewind #2

Now let's rewind the tape on this engagement. Customer B tells me he needs his graphic by Friday. Let's make it Tuesday that this conversation is happening. If I'm a salesperson for a company like Olympus Group, I'm probably not empowered to commit to something like this without checking with the production side of the business – and I *shouldn't* commit blindly, even if what the customer needs fits easily with normal turnaround parameters. That's a different case, though, and I'll come back to that in just a moment.

In this case, I would say: "Let me check with production. I'll be back to you ASAP." (ASAP, by the way, probably needs to be PDQ – Pretty Damn Quick! Time is always relative. If you're talking something with plenty of lead time, tomorrow – or even later – might be quick enough. If you're talking about something on a fast turnaround, end-of-day-today might be too slow!)

So I check with Production, and get the good news/bad news. I can accept the order if we get paid for the overtime. I would not, though, lead with that when I re-engage with Customer B. Instead, I would say: "I'm still working on getting a commitment for a Friday delivery. It's looking like we probably can. But let me ask you, if we need another day, which in this case would mean delivering by end-of-day on Monday, could that work for you?"

Sounds like the same conversation I posed earlier, right? But it's not, because no one has mentioned overtime or additional cost. And that allows for the possibility that this negative topic will never have to come up. (Do you agree, by the way, that it's better if it doesn't?) The best-case-scenario here is that Customer B still says: "Sure, I can live with that."

The worst-case-scenario is that he clings to his want. OK, now we have to talk about additional cost, and we'll see how much value a Friday delivery really has to this particular customer in this particular situation. I've seen people say *no* to the initial question, but then say *yes* when faced with a cost attached. I have also seen people say: "I understand, and I'm happy to pay the overtime to make sure that I have it on Friday." There's a range of response here. My point is to try to position for the best-case-scenario.

Having said that, you can't be afraid to ask for the overtime if that's what it's going to take. Or to ask for whatever price you have to charge to deliver on what they want or what they need. Remember, the best way to be able to overcome a price objection is to be able to say: *This is how much you'll have to spend in order to get what you've told me that you want or need.*

Rewind #3

Let's rewind the tape one more time. Did it occur to you that I could have asked the "if we need another day" question even before ending that stage of the engagement? I could have asked: "When do you need it?" He could have said: "I need it by Friday!" I could have said: "I will talk to Production. But before I do, if it turns out that we need another day…"

Here's how the follow-up engagement might then have gone: "Friday is a possible. Monday is a definite. Do we have your approval to move forward with the order based on that commitment?"

Again, this avoids any need to talk about additional charges. It also avoids any need to ask anyone to work any overtime. Yes, as I noted, some of that time-and-a-half might have been appreciated, but maybe not. I always prefer to save any sort of schedule disruption for when I really need it.

Different Case

I mentioned earlier that you should never commit *blindly* to a delivery commitment – or any other commitment, for that matter – even if it falls well within normal or reasonable standards or expectations. To explain that, let me tell you a story.

A few years ago, I was placing an order with one of my own suppliers. It was a situation where what I was asking for was very reasonable, and there was plenty of time to get it done. I think 99% of the salespeople in the world would have said "No Problem!"

This particular salesperson took a different approach: "I'm 90% sure we can do that," she said. "But let me check to make 100% sure, and if I see any problem, I'll call you before the end of the day."

At around 4:00 PM, my phone rang, and it was the salesperson. "Mr. Fellman," she said, "I promised I'd call if I found any problem with getting you what you want when you want it. I checked with my people, and unless something completely unforeseen comes up, we'll have it to you then. And in fact, if it turns out that we can get it there sooner, will you be ready to take it?"

Think about what transpired here. First, the salesperson differentiated herself by not giving me a shallow, typical, salesperson response. Second, she implied that I'd only hear from her if there was a problem, but then she called anyway to confirm that everything looked good. Third, she qualified her response by saying "unless anything completely unforeseen comes up." Fourth, she presented an early delivery as a possibility without making a commitment to it, setting up the situation where she could "under-promise then over-perform."

Fifth, the last thing she said to me was: "OK, Mr. Fellman, don't hesitate to call me if you have any questions between now and then, and you can be sure I'll be calling you if anything unforeseen comes up." As it turned out, she didn't have to call me with bad news, though she did call me the day after the delivery to make sure that I was happy.

I've mentioned before that little things can make big differences. In fact, I have long believed that the biggest difference between good companies and great companies (and of course, not-so-good companies) doesn't relate to any one big thing. It's really that the great companies master the little things that do make big differences. To me, this is a story about six little things that added up to one big thing — a happy customer!

No Problem

While I'm on this subject, I'd like to recommend that you take that phrase "No Problem" and remove it completely from your vocabulary. OK, maybe I'm nitpicking here, but "No Problem" has become such a common part of our vernacular that I'm pretty sure I hear it 40-50 times a day, usually as a response to "Thank You!"

Now, think about exactly what you're saying if a customer says "Thank You" and you answer "No Problem" — *"I was willing to do this thing for you because it didn't inconvenience me at all!"* Is that really the message you're hoping to communicate? The proper response, I think, is *"You're welcome"* or maybe better still: *"You're very welcome and I was happy to do it for you because I appreciate your business!"*

Creative Persistence

As I wrote earlier, *persistence* is generally considered to be a positive attribute for a salesperson. I draw a distinction, though, between what I call *blind persistence* and a more creative form. I suspect you've been on the receiving end of blind persistence – a salesperson who calls and calls and emails and calls without adding anything of value to the relationship. I suspect that, by now, you delete his or her phone messages and/or emails pretty quickly.

The first step toward creative persistence is to formulate a plan. That involves a series of questions:

1. Where am I now?
2. What is my immediate goal?
3. How long should I allow myself to get there?
4. What do I do first, then next, then next, etc?

Here's a plan I worked out with one of my clients a few months ago. His answer to the first question was "a high-value suspect, but I haven't been able to get him to respond to an introductory email and my immediate follow-up" His answer to the second question was "a face-to-face meeting." His answer to the third question was "like, now!", but I asked him if that seemed reasonable. I suggested that he give himself three months, and then we started talking about the fourth question.

The ultimate plan involved six "touches" over three months. The first touch was an email, to be sent on Day 1 of the program. "I have been trying pretty hard to connect with you to set up a meeting. Obviously, you're not in any hurry to do that. I think I can bring value, though, and I don't want to give up on you, so here's what I'd like to propose. Please keep your eye on your in-basket, both email and snail mail, for a couple of things I'm going to be sending you. Hopefully, I will convince you that meeting with me is a good idea."

The second touch, planned for two weeks later, was to send a sample of material to the suspect. (I should mention that my client's product has to stand up to rough treatment, and the product itself far too large and expensive to be sent as a sample/demo.) The sample of material was accompanied by a short note: "I thought this was a good way to start the conversation I'd like to have with you. This is the material our product is made of. As you can see, it's tough stuff!"

Here's an important part of this plan. There was no "call to action." No request for a meeting, no request for a phone or email response. The intent was a "light" touch – which is the exact opposite of most blind persistence, wouldn't you agree?

Here's another important part of the plan. The sample was a block of the material, measuring 12" x 18" x 3", and packaged in black, heavyweight shrink-wrap. It definitely had some "what's this?" appeal!

The third touch, scheduled for two weeks after that, was an email that contained technical specs of the material, again with a short note – and no call to action! "This is to follow up on the material sample I sent you two weeks ago. Here you'll see the technical specs, which I hope will support my contention that it's *tough stuff!*"

The fourth touch, scheduled for two weeks after that, was another email, containing a link to a page at my client's website which featured a case-study on the product." The body of the email said: "I thought you might find this interesting." Again, no call to action other than the implicit action suggested by the link.

The fifth touch, this time at a three week interval, was a baseball cap, embroidered with my client's logo, sent through the mail with another short note – "I thought you might enjoy having this" – and again, no call to action.

The sixth touch, three weeks later – and three months from the first touch! – was a phone call. "I am hoping that the materials I've sent you over the last few months have created enough interest to sit down with me for a face-to-face meeting. What do you think?"

Success Story?

OK, I probably wouldn't have told this story if it didn't work. It did result in a face-to-face meeting, although it has not yet resulted in a sale. I'm not going to promise you, though, that this sort of creative persistence will always work for you. Experience has shown that it doesn't. But I do think it's a better strategy than calling and calling and emailing and calling, etc.

Keep asking yourself: *"How can I bring value to my persistence?* Or if not value, at least creativity. And: *"How can I build the relationship I'm hoping to build, one piece –* one *engagement – at a time?"*

The Point Of Sale

We've covered a lot of ground since Chapter One, where I (hopefully) established that much of the sales engagement process can occur well before the participants reach The Point of Sale, through effective advertising. I stressed, in fact, that engagement *is* a process, which means that it's usually best accomplished in steps or stages. The first stage of suspect engagement via advertising is to capture attention. The second stage is to establish interest. The third stage, if interest is indeed present, is to motivate action – in other words, to create movement toward The Point Of Sale. That might mean *into the store* (in the case of *retail* advertising), or *into the funnel* (in the case of *commercial* advertising). It might mean into a brick-and-mortar or other face-to-face (or voice-to-voice) situation, or it might mean a *click/ visit* to your website. Either way, that advertising engagement can ultimately take us to one of only three results:

1. Qualification – When we learn that they really are qualified prospects for what we sell, and worth pursuing.
2. Disqualification – When we learn that they aren't, for whatever reason.
3. New Customer! – When they actually buy something, pretty much immediately, at the store or from the funnel.

Earlier in this chapter, I noted that the ongoing process of turning a qualified prospect into a customer can be:

*   Short and Easy
*   Short and Hard
*   Long and Easy
*   Long and Hard

I should have added another possibility: *Impossible.* (Actually, I did sort of make that point in Chapter One, and again in Chapter Four. I wrote that you can't sell to everyone, even the *fully qualified prospects* who engage with you at The Point of Sale. I wish you could. I wish *I* could! But that's an unreasonable – and therefore unhealthy – expectation.)

OK, you can't sell to everyone. Sometimes it just isn't in the cards. Sometimes they decide on a different option – a different product or a different supplier. Sometimes you, as a salesperson, just get outsold! Remember that *selling is all about helping people to make the decision to buy from you.* Sometimes, someone else just does that better. If that happens to you, please embrace the opportunity to learn from the experience, to minimize the likelihood of it happening again!

Sometimes, though, Salesperson B gets the *yes* because Salesperson A (that would be you!) commits the Cardinal Selling Sin of not asking for the *yes.* To me, that's not being outsold, it's not even competing!

That raises a question. Are you a *reluctant salesperson*? One of my colleagues uses that term to describe people who find themselves in the sales role, not because they want to be, but because they have to be. This is often situational – as I noted earlier, *salesperson* describes anyone who is doing any of the things we've defined as *selling*, at least during any engagement during which they are doing and of those things.

I've observed that many reluctant salespeople can handle two of the three elements of *professional selling* just fine – remember knowledge, integrity and convincing skills? Knowledge? Check! Integrity? Check! Convincing skills? Ouch!

So here's a little secret. Convincing skills are overrated. Sometimes, all you have to do to get the *yes* is to ask for the *yes*. And if you don't get the *yes*, sometimes all you have to do is ask *why*? I have a favorite way of framing it when I find myself in a *why* situation: *"Can I ask you, what's keeping you from saying 'yes' to me right now?"* It's not a demand, right? It's a question! I like to think that it's *assertive* but not *pushy*. And I have found that I often get an honest, thoughtful answer – which, when coupled with *your* knowledge and integrity, might make it pretty easy for *you* to address the objection and get the *yes* on a subsequent try.

Here's a statistic that I can't prove, but I believe it to be at least ballpark-true. A salesperson with top-notch convincing skills might get to *yes* with qualified prospects 75% of the time. A salesperson with *good* convincing skills might get to *yes* with qualified prospects 50% of the time. A reluctant salesperson with zero confidence in his or her convincing skills might get to *yes* with qualified prospects 40% of the time – if he or she is willing to ask for the *yes* in the first place, and ask *why* if that *yes* is not immediately forthcoming. John Lennon said that all you need is love. I'm saying that all you need to be an *effective* salesperson is knowledge, integrity and maybe a little courage.

One final thought on asking for the *yes* in the first place. I found an interesting blog entry on hubspot.com, written by Emma Brudner, and titled 25 Closing Phrases to Seal a Sales Deal in 2020. Among them were:

- "Is there any reason, if we gave you the product at this price, that you wouldn't do business with our company?"
- "If we throw in [freebie], would that convince you to sign the contract today?"

- "I'd hate to see [negative consequence] befall your company because you didn't have the right product in place. Do you want to take the crucial step to protect your organization today?"
- "It seems like [product] is a good fit for [company]. What do you think?"

I strongly recommend that you disregard every word of that, except for the last four words. To me, a sales engagement has two main elements, the needs/wants assessment we discussed earlier, and the salesperson's proposal or recommendation. That proposal/recommendation boils down to: *"This is what I think."* Doesn't that make the obvious closing question: "W*hat do you think?"*

OK, I think it's time to hear from Brian again.

8 Communication and Connection
Brian Adam

"I wish my company communicated less with me. They keep sharing useful information all the time and I want them to stop."

This quote was attributed to "Author Unknown" but I think it was really "Author Nonexistent" – because I don't believe any employee has ever actually said these words! In my experience most employees believe that their company's communication could improve. In one way or another, we all crave more information. We want to know what's going on, how we're doing, how the company is doing. We want to know if our manager(s) think we're doing a good job. We want to know what the company's plans are, and what's happening with key customers. We want to know who that new employee is, and where he/she works. We want to know what we don't know that might be important to us!

At Olympus, we are very aware of the challenges of communicating effectively with our employees. I recently conducted a survey on our company culture, and "communication" was the category our employees rated us the worst at. They felt we could do a better job of sharing more information, and that they would benefit from us sharing "the whole picture."

That stung a little, as I have made a very conscious effort to communicate effectively. I thought I *was* sharing the whole picture! But feedback is a gift, right? I took this feedback to heart, asked our team for clarification, and walked away with a clear understanding that I was not doing as great a job as I thought with our corporate communication.

This is a challenging topic, in part due to its complexity. "Effective communication" is a broad and ambiguous term. It can mean very different things to different people. In fact, that's probably the key lesson we learned from our survey. Obviously it was important to learn that, in general, our team was not satisfied with the level of communication, but learning what "effective" meant to different people was equally important.

Here's what we heard from different people with different job responsibilities and/or work situations:

Individual	What "Effective Communication" Means To Them
Accountant	Accurate financials and detailed forecasts
Press Operator	Detailed and accurate work orders/instructions
New Parent	Clearly articulated overview of maternity/paternity leave policy
Salesperson	Understanding marketing strategy and knowledge of differentiators
New Employee	Clear understanding of benefits
Everybody	Feedback on their performance – *Am I doing a good job?*

We all have different needs and desires when it comes to communication. Some of us want an incredible amount of detail, and want to know exactly what's going on in every facet of the business. Others may simply want to know the strategic direction – the high-level plans – and their managers' feedback on their performance. Still others may only want to know what they have to do every day to keep their jobs. (That's not the level of engagement we're looking for, though, is it?)

To achieve that kind of engagement, it's critical that "effective" communication happens with every one of these individuals. The accountant gets accurate numbers. The press operator gets a detailed work order. The new parent gets help in understanding HR policy details. The salesperson gets training, to be able to understand and articulate the company's differentiators. The new employee gets a solid onboarding and ongoing communication to understand the benefit offerings, and *everybody* is provided with a clear understanding of what's expected of them, plus feedback on their performance.

In my experience, all of this is much easier said than done. But it needs to be done! So how do we rise to the challenge?

Use Multiple Channels

First, use more than one channel of communication to broaden the reach of your message.

Take a moment to think about the different ways we consume news today. My father reads a newspaper, my mother watches the news on TV, my wife reads cnn.com, my brother listens to a podcast (the Daily), and I spend a lot of time on LinkedIn. (I also like to read the Economist when I'm traveling.) Here are five people, all from the same family, who have completely different preferences on how we like to receive and digest our news.

Think of all of the channels of communication available today:

- Newspapers
- LinkedIn
- Evening News on TV
- Twitter
- Word of mouth
- Facebook
- Podcast
- Newsletters
- YouTube
- Religious groups (sermons)
- CNN & other 24-hour news channels
- Apps on your phone
- Magazines
- Countless others that I'm forgetting or don't even know of yet

In the workplace, we are trying to share "news" with everyone on our team every day. Our team members use all of these different communication channels every day, and likely have very different preferences on how *they* prefer to get their news – both inside and outside of work. So one very important key to an effective corporate communication strategy is to use as many different channels as possible.

But, you may be thinking, if I *share* the same message again and again won't employees *hear* the exact same message again and again? Yes and this is exactly what you want! I attended a public speaking seminar a couple of years ago, and our instructor, LaQuita Cleare, shared some great advice that really resonated with me.

"There's a common belief that an individual must hear something seven times before they will remember it," she said. "So if you've shared the same message four times, don't get frustrated. Get excited! You're more than halfway there, and now you only have to repeat your message three more times until they will remember it."

This piece of advice completely changed my outlook on communication. I no longer get frustrated when someone doesn't remember something that I told them *once*. Instead, I now recognize that I need to repeat the message multiple times. This was also a great justification for sharing the same news via multiple communication channels. I just view each channel as *one* step closer to the *seven* times I need to share an individual bit of information.

Now, this is not to say that we repeat every single thing seven times at Olympus, but we have definitely taken LaQuita's advice. We are *focused* on using multiple channels to share news with our teams. Here are examples of the different channels we use:

- Monthly Newsletter – We produce two versions of our company newsletter every month, both a traditional printed version and a digital version that we distribute by email. We highlight results, ask different divisions and teams to provide updates, introduce new hires, "shout out" our superstars, recognize birthdays and report on the status of those Hey Brian! suggestions I mentioned earlier. We even translate a summary of the newsletter into Spanish and Hmong for our employees who are more comfortable in these languages.
- Emails – In between newsletters, we send your typical email updates, keeping our team members apprised on a variety of topics. In addition, I've adopted a best practice from a good friend of mine. Riley Didion runs a complex food processing business – Didion Mills – and he is all about *rhythm* in his life and in everything he does. A couple of years ago, Riley introduced me to his "Monday Morning Update" routine. Every Monday morning, he sends out an email to his entire team. The topics vary. One week he might describe a cool project they are working on. The next week might be an update on

company results. He has used the Monday Morning Update to address various rumors that seem to be circulating, to introduce new team members and to share tips and tricks to improve efficiency. I loved the idea, and now our employees have come to expect an email from me every Monday morning. The *rhythm* of doing this every Monday morning makes it a *habit,* and our Monday Morning Update has become a particular method of communication that our employees appreciate.

- Town Hall Meetings – We hold quarterly meetings with each department (groups of 5-15). In these meetings, I share a high-level overview of corporate results, update our team on major projects/ initiatives, address any rumors and reiterate important facets of our culture. Side note – I believe "all hands" meetings are quite common across many organizations. In other words, pull the entire team together and provide a high-level update to everyone at the same time. We used to do all-hands meetings at Olympus too, with remote offices video-conferencing in. A couple of years ago we switched to the smaller, departmental meetings, and we found the format of these smaller groups to be far more engaging. It allowed us to address concerns or topics that are only relevant to a subset of our employees, and it also made it easier for us to translate into other languages for employees who are more comfortable in a language other than English.

- Bulletin Boards/TV Screens in Lunchrooms – We installed TV screens in each location's lunchroom. They are primarily used to communicate via slideshows, everything from daily news to corporate updates, announcing new hires, sharing feedback from customers and providing a snapshot on high-level metrics. Essentially, this gives us a small internal newsfeed and allows us to show appreciation *and* to reiterate key messages. We've found it to be a pretty inexpensive and easy tool to provide real-time updates.

- MBWA – Management By Wandering Around – Another of my favorite communication strategies is simply to walk around our facilities, talking with team members as I go. This is nothing more than old-fashioned, word-of-mouth communication. I have found it to be a great way to learn what's on people's minds – and also to discover what rumors might be circulating, and to get a feel for the general demeanor of the team. This also helps build the connections I want with our team members. (More on MBWA, connections and engagement to follow.)

- Communication Centers – We have established large communication centers at each of our facilities. These are basically multi-panel bulletin boards where we post all kinds of information, including KPIs (Key Performance Indicators), PTO schedules, photos of cool projects we're executing for our customers and status on major internal projects and initiatives. We update these weekly, and we also hold our weekly department production meetings in front of the communication centers.
- Wiki/Internal Websites – We recently launched a simple internal website, and all of our employees have access to it. It's easily searchable, and a great repository for the countless updates and forms that every business has.

If you count 'em up, you'll see that I've listed seven separate communication channels. Now the arithmetic is pretty simple. If we share each important message via each of these unique channels, we've hit LaQuita Cleare's magical "Hey, they might remember this!" number, and significantly increased the likelihood of *effective communication* with our entire team.

Share (Almost) Everything

The phrase "Open Book Management" was coined by John Case of Inc. Magazine in 1993. Case believed that a company performs best when people view themselves as partners, rather than as numbers or hired help. I love this concept. When you think about it from an employee engagement perspective, who is more likely to be highly engaged?

- *Hired Help* – Someone who views themselves as a headcount or a number inside a giant machine.

- *Partner* – Someone who feels like they have a stake in the business, and who's *in the loop* on all important decisions.

The idea behind Open Book Management is to share all relevant financial information about the company with employees. That includes sales volume, profit, cash flow and expenses. It doesn't have to include *everything* – for example, I don't feel that my employees need to know my salary, or anyone else's for that matter – but within reason, I want to be far more open than closed.

Case hit the nail right on the head, as far as I'm concerned. *Information* contributes to *engagement*. And, by the way, it also enables your employees to make better decisions on your company's behalf!

Jack Stack, CEO of SRC Holdings and author of *The Great Game of Business*, is probably the best-known example of Case's open book management concept. Stack turned a small struggling truck engine manufacturer around – into a $1 billion holding company with over 1,600 employees! He opened up the company's books, ensuring that everyone understood how they made money, and what each individual could do to impact the results. The book is a great read, and it inspired me to try my own hand at financial literacy with my team.

Here's how I started. A couple of years ago, at one of our quarterly town hall meetings, I asked our employees this question:

"If we sell a banner for $100, how much profit do we make? How much is left over after all our expenses are accounted for?"

The answers were pretty illuminating. They ranged from $1 all the way up to $75 in profit. Most of the answers were between $10 and $30.

So what is the correct answer? I'm not sure I really intended to share all of this with you when we started this project, but I guess it's part of being an open book, right? Over the past ten years, we have averaged about 5% gross profit. In our best years, we got close to 10%. In our worst years, we were at or below zero.

My point in sharing this, by the way, is not to discourage anyone from entering the printing industry – although I wouldn't blame you if you sought greener pastures! What I really want to do is simply illustrate the poor job I had done communicating with our employees. They were not aware of how thin our profit margins were, and along with that, how small our margin for error truly was.

Based on this feedback, I decided to harness Case's and Stack's principles and build some higher level financial literacy with our team. Knowing that I was starting from a very low level of understanding, I wanted to make it as simple and direct as possible. So I walked into our follow-up meeting with $100 in singles and laid them on the table.

"Here's our revenue from that $100 banner sale," I said. "Now, let me show you where the money goes."

I then took the money and counted it into four separate piles, explaining each category as I went along:

- Materials $20
- Labor $20
- Overhead $30 (presses, sewing machines, building)
- SG&A $25 (computers, marketing, HR, sales, accounting)

When I finished with that, I held the last $5 in my hand. "At the end of the day, on a $100 sale, we make about $5. Now let me show you where *that* goes."

I then took those last 5 singles and counted them into three piles:

- $2 – We pay this in taxes
- $2 – We reinvest this in the business
- $1 – This goes back to you as part of our profit sharing plan (more on that to follow)

Just about everyone seemed surprised at just how little money we actually made on a "typical" order. But I wasn't done yet. I had two more important points I wanted to make.

"Now let's take a look at what happens when we make a mistake. Let's say we have to remake a banner. In this scenario, our customer still pays us $100, but now we have double the material cost and double the labor cost."

I pulled the $100 in singles back together, and then started counting out piles again:

- Materials $40
- Labor $40
- Overhead $30 (presses, sewing machines, building)
- SG&A $25 (computers, marketing, HR, sales, accounting)

At $20 into the overhead, I ran out of singles, so I reached into my pocket to "borrow" money from the profit we'd earned on other jobs – $10 more to cover the rest of the overhead and $25 to cover SG&A.

"If we make a mistake, we stand to lose $35 on this $100 sale. Then we need to sell 7 more $100 jobs at $5 in profit just to get back to zero!"

The looks on their faces showed me that I'd gotten through to them. It was a very powerful message, illustrating the cost of mistakes to our team.

But I still wasn't done. "Let's talk about what happens if we find ways to work smarter. Here's the starting point. Our customer will pay us $100 for the banner, regardless of how long it takes us to produce it or how much material we use. They want their banner done right and delivered on time. How we do that is completely up to us."

I pulled all the singles together again, and started counting out new piles, again, explaining as I went:

- Materials $15 ($5 in savings achieved by "nesting" materials)
- Labor $10 ($10 in savings achieved by working more efficiently)
- Overhead $30 (no change here)
- SG&A $25 (no change here either)

At this point, I still had $20 in my hand. "Look at this," I said. "By working smarter and more efficiently, we could increase the profit on a job like this to $20. Now let me show you where *that* would go."

- $8 – We pay this in taxes
- $8 – We reinvest this in the business
- $4 – This goes back to you as part of our profit sharing plan – 4X the original amount!

Again, the looks on their faces showed that I'd gotten through to them. But it is worth asking, *should you really share information on how much money your company is making with your employees?*

Obviously, I think you should. I believe this is a critical step in improving engagement. Employees want to know the "whole picture," and if you're a "for profit" business, your profitability is part of that picture. If you don't share this kind of information, I worry that your employees will draw their own picture of how profitable you are, and what you are doing with all that money. They might create images of big fancy yachts or private jets – and I can tell you, at 5% profit margins, this certainly is not happening in my life anytime soon!

At Olympus, we take this a step further. Not only do we share how much money we make, we also show our team members what we spend our profits on. Now, we do this at "overview" level. I don't try to explain how depreciation schedules for large CapEx purchases work. But I do want our team members to know that we are reinvesting in the business, and that they're not simply busting their butts to put money in my pocket.

Here's a hypothetical example of the level of detail as we share this sort of information with our employees:

Pre-Tax Profit:	**$1,800,000**
Taxes:	**$700,000**
Reinvested in the Business:	**$750,000**

- New UV Digital Presses & Automated Cutter $450,000
- Facility Upgrades $125,000
- Computer Upgrades $50,000
- New Website - $50,000
- Employee Tuition Reimbursement Program $75,000

Profit Sharing:	**$350,000**

As you can see, this is done in "round numbers," but it's still pretty transparent. I want our employees to feel like they earned these profits and benefitted from them. Even the taxes, which provide for some of the services we enjoy on a local, state and national basis. I'm pretty sure that this level of transparency has increased engagement, and helped to align the entire team around a common mission and purpose.

Now, there will inevitably be times when you'll want to – or be legally required to – keep things closer to vest. For example, liquidity events (if you're planning on selling your business), anything that involves NDA's (non-disclosure agreements), or Personal Data (such as anything related to HIPPA). But I believe that the vast majority of what most companies keep "close to the vest" actually does more harm than good, at least from an employee engagement perspective.

Strategic Plan

When we talked with our team about "the whole picture," they made it clear that they're more interested in the future than in the past. That's worth thinking about. I think you know from my introduction that I'm very proud of Olympus's history. I am also very proud of the culture we have established, and our reputation, both with our customers and within our industry. But all of that has already happened. As the old saying goes, what have you done for me lately? And what are you going to do for me tomorrow?

Turns out it's not just customers who ask those questions. It's employees too, especially the question about tomorrow!

The future is best represented by your strategic plan. Where are you headed? How do you hope to get there? These are questions of concern to your best employees. And their buy-in is important to you – which is not to say that you have to have 100% *agreement* in order to be successful, but at the very least, you want a high degree of *alignment*. That starts with *understanding*. Think about how easy it could be to have everyone rowing in opposite directions if they don't know the desired direction in the first place! Alignment around high-level goals is key to teamwork.

High-level, by the way, doesn't mean *the goals of high-level people*. Think of it this way. You might set a goal to increase your sales by 25%. In support of that goal, you might establish three *component* goals:

1. Introduce a new website, along with an advertising program to draw people to it

2. Hire and train three new salespeople
3. Add a second shift to increase production capacity

For each of those component goals, you will probably have some number of *sub-component* goals. In other words, each level is supported by its own component goals. Increasing sales by 25% is a top-level, company-wide goal. It is supported by three second-level, department-wide goals. In turn, each of those is supported by third-level and maybe even lower-level goals and plans that take us down to small teams or even individual people. *High-level* is relative to each individual. If I'm one of those individual people with a role to play in support of a goal, my specific role is a high-level goal for me!

EOS

At Olympus, we are an EOS company, EOS stands for the Entrepreneur's Operating System. It's a business framework developed by Gino Wickman, the author of *Traction*. The book is a great read, and helps small business stay focused and organized. It applies a series of simple and useful tools around *structure, meeting rhythm* and *communication*.

Meeting rhythm all by itself is worth talking about. It's pretty well accepted that most organizations hold too many meetings that waste too many people's time. But EOS believes that well-run meetings are "the moment of truth" for accountability. *Well-run*, of course, is the key phrase.

Meeting Rhythm is all about optimizing your meetings, by:

- Having regularly scheduled meetings on a clockwork cadence
- Having the right attendees in the meetings
- Having a written agenda for the meetings
- Having a definite start time
- Having a definite stop time

As we've learned, it's not about having fewer meetings, it's about having *better* meetings.

Beyond that, one of the most impactful things we have taken from EOS is its version of a strategic plan, which is called the VTO, or Vision-Traction Organizer. It's a simple, one-page format which is shared with every single employee, and updated every quarter. I can't stress enough how useful a tool this has been for our team.

Our version of the VTO includes the following:

- **Our BHAG** – Big Hairy Audacious Goal – a concept I took from another book, "Built To Last: Successful Habits of Visionary Companies" by Jim Collins and Jerry Porras. A BHAG is defined as a long-term goal that everyone in a company can understand and rally behind – and it's meant to be a grandiose, earth-moving goal. Our BHAG is to pay out $1 million in profit sharing to our team members.
- **Our Long-Term Vision** – where are we headed and how will we get there?
- **Our 1-year Plan** – along with 90-day goals/projects
- **Our Scorecard** – how we are performing against our KPI's (Key Performance Indicators/Metrics)
- **Our Culture** – we also included aspects of our culture including Core Purpose and Core Values

As noted, we update our strategic plan every quarter, then we share it as part of our town hall meetings with every single team member. This allows me to meet with every employee and to focus on four things:

- How we are doing
- Where we are going
- How we are going to get there
- How you can help

If you walk around one of our facilities today, you'll see our quarterly plan posted at individual employees' workstations throughout every department. It's pretty cool to walk around and see how much pride our team members take in being included in our strategic plan.

One final thought regarding EOS. It has given us numerous other tools that have positively impacted our organization, but the strategic plan has had the most significant impact on our employee engagement.

Building Connections

Connecting with individual employees is a critical step in developing high levels of engagement. In order to manage, motivate, coach or lead effectively, you must take the time to understand and *connect* with your team members. And it isn't easy! It takes focus and effort, and it often takes a lot of time, but without strong relationships and connections, you simply cannot expect to reach anything close to max engagement.

So here's a quick secret to jump starting your connections. If you only remember one thing from this entire book that will improve your level of engagement – not just with employees but with everyone in your life – it can be summed up in one simple four-letter word: **CARE!**

If you truly care about your employees, your co-workers or your teammates, you will instantly improve your connections with them. It's tough to fake. You actually do have to care about others. You have to take a vested interest in their success and their well-being. You have to make and take the time to get to know them, both professionally and personally. So how do you demonstrate this sort of care and start building closer connections?

First, let me back up a moment to the idea that it's tough to fake. If you really *don't* care about your employees, we have a problem. But it's not an unsolvable problem. Care, it turns out, is an attribute that can be practiced and perfected. First, you need to recognize that you may be deficient in this area, and it hinders your ability to lead a successful team – or a successful business! Next, you have to commit to this area of personal growth. Then, you fake it till you make it!

I'm not being flippant here. I believe that, if you show interest in your people, you will find that they are interesting. As you get to know them better, you will find that you do care. OK, probably not with everybody, but with enough to improve your situation.

Think back on what I wrote earlier about my Monday Morning Update, about how the rhythm of doing it every Monday made it a habit. Here's my recommendation. Start *acting* like you care, and see where that takes you. I wouldn't be surprised if you can start building a *caring habit*.

Getting To Know Them

I wrote earlier about how we do "hypothetical" exit interviews with current employees, and how one of the questions that I like to ask in those conversations is: *"What would you do if you won the lottery?"*

I have found this to be a great question, because it really asks team members to share their aspirations and dreams. Typical answers include buying a house, paying back student loans, taking an extended, luxurious vacation and buying a dream car.

We had an employee named Tina (not her real name), a super creative individual who worked in our mascot department. On Tina's one-year anniversary, I sat down with her for our hypothetical exit interview. When I asked her what she'd do if she won the lottery, I got an unexpected response.

"Brian," she said, "if I won the lottery, I'd pay off my student loans, take a trip, and then you know what I'd do? I'd buy a stainless-steel garbage can. You know, those fancy ones that open automatically."

"Tina, why a garbage can?" I asked "Can you please explain? I'm curious to know more."

"Well," she said, "I just have the cheap plastic garbage cans in my apartment. But those stainless-steel ones, those are classy. That's how you know you've made it."

I think Tina was half-joking, but I took note of her response. Then, a couple of months later, we had a major project for one of our biggest mascot customers, with a very tight deadline that looked like it was at risk. Tina made some significant personal sacrifices to come in over the weekend to fabricate this mascot, and she crushed it. She produced a high-quality mascot, in spite of a tough deadline, and our customer was ecstatic.

Her supervisor gave her Monday off. On Tuesday when she got to work, next to her workstation was a stainless-steel garbage can with a bow on top and a note from me. *"It's not quite winning the lottery but thanks for winning over a key customer. Truly appreciate your hard work and hitting a tough deadline!"*

Every conversation with a team member gives you an opportunity to learn something about them. And sometimes, those little bits of personal knowledge lead to an even more meaningful connection. Whether it comes from a planned conversation like this hypothetical exit interview, or a random conversation in the break room or on the shop floor, pay attention, and make it a point to remember these personal details. I have no question that my ability – learned from Tina! – to give her a very personal thank you gift contributed to a very solid connection for as long as she worked for us.

Here's another example, this one from our Orlando office, I was having lunch with an employee named Steve (again not his real name). Steve is the teammate that everybody simply loves. He has a great attitude, he'll do anything you need him to do, and always has everyone's back. We once gave Steve a spot bonus for working over a weekend, and the next week an ice cream truck stopped at our facility. Free ice cream for everybody. Steve had arranged the whole thing. He decided to spend his entire bonus to buy ice cream for the whole team! With that generous, kind gesture, Steve even strengthened his connection to his teammates.

At our lunch, I asked Steve the lottery question, and he told me that he always wanted to go to Ireland. It was on his bucket list, but he had never pulled the trigger and booked a ticket. After just a little bit of thought, I decided that Olympus would buy his ticket to Ireland. Again, a very personal thank you gift. I mean, this is a guy who took his last reward from Olympus and spent it on his teammates. We value him, and want to keep him engaged.

Please don't miss the point of this story, though. It's not about what a great guy I am for sending Steve to Ireland. It's about the *connection* that resulted from the *conversation*, from me showing interest *in* him and learning something interesting *about* him.

Management by Wandering Around

Another thing I wrote about earlier – and promised to come back to – was MBWA. One of the simplest ways of improving connections is perhaps the oldest management tactic, walking around the workplace and talking with employees. The "high concept" of Management By Wandering Around was popularized in 1970's and 1980's by Bill Hewlett and David Packard, the founders of Hewlett-Packard. Steve Jobs of Apple was another well-known practitioner. The idea is that walking around a workplace helps you connect with employees, improves the sharing of ideas, invites suggestions, and opens your eyes to what's happening (or perhaps not happening). It's very similar to the Japanese GEMBA Walk developed at Toyota. By walking "aimlessly" around, you'll have informal conversations and therefore build better connections and higher levels of engagement.

(Some managers – and Business professors – seem to object to the idea of "aimless" wandering. That's why you'll sometimes see MBWA defined as Management By *Walking* Around. Personally, I see value in both aimed and aimless, so call it whatever you want!)

My father, Helmut, was a big proponent of MBWA. He would do daily rounds, always finding reasons to pop into offices and work areas, specifically to promote those informal interactions.

I'll never forget that, when my father bought Olympus in 1991, the company was in trouble. It was on the brink of bankruptcy and things needed to change, fast! One of Helmut's very first actions was to ditch the CEO's corner office. Instead, he put his desk smack dab in the middle of the facility – no walls, no windows, no fancy office. It was an unconventional move at the time, when most executives coveted their *executive privilege* (private bathrooms, reserved parking spots, corner offices, etc.) But Helmut felt that he needed to dive into the nerve center of the organization, where the real work happened. He put himself amongst his team members, amongst the problems and issues and amongst the action. This gave him clear vision and insight into what needed to change, and helped him connect with his team.

I don't think Helmut used the same terminology – the term "employee engagement" wasn't quite in vogue yet – but he was very intentionally focusing on *engaging* with employees and attempting to build improved connections all throughout the team. And you know what, it worked! I like to think that his focus on fostering and building these connections was a key factor in his ability to transform Olympus, from a failing company on the brink of bankruptcy to a profitable organization.

A quick aside, to address one of my own core beliefs. Another action Helmut took as soon as he acquired Olympus was to remove the "reserved" parking spots. No longer did the C-suite players get the best parking spots. He felt this "hierarchy" negatively affected engagement by creating a class system within a company. When he was questioned about removing the reserved spaces, I loved his justification: "If you want the best parking spot, get here first."

My belief is that *executive privilege* inhibits your ability to build strong connections and decreases your ability to connect. I believe in *executive responsibility* to connect.

Lessons Learned

I also believe in *executive responsibility* to learn from mistakes. At Olympus, we've made our share. For example, one of our biggest *connection* problems was that we used to classify our employees as either *Salary* or *Hourly*. *Salary* employees were executives, managers and office employees, while production employees made up most of the *Hourly* category. We used to offer completely different perks and benefits for hourly and salary employees.

Hourly	Salary
15 days of vacation	18 days of vacation
No sick days	3 sick days
In-office holiday luncheon	Formal holiday party at country club
Tardy policy with point system	No tardy policy

Believe it or not, the biggest problem with this policy was the holiday party. It got to the point where we were altering peoples' *Hourly* vs *Salary* status just so they could attend our formal, off-site party, and that had an unintended result of impacting overtime pay. Yes, it was getting a bit ridiculous, and there is no way the hierarchy could have been helpful in improving connections.

So what did we do? We standardized our policy on sick time, vacation and PTO. We combined the holiday parties into one event. We did away with the point system. And I vowed to never publish a traditional organizational chart. Has this transformed our business? No. But has it increased the likelihood that an hourly employee will feel connected to me, and therefore more highly engaged? I think that it has.

It's Not Rocket Science!

Back to MBWA. So how do you do it? Wandering around is certainly not rocket science, but it does require a bit of thought – and a certain amount of diligence. Here are a couple of tips to build MBWA into your daily routine.

- **Schedule the time** – Until it becomes a habit, you probably will need to put forth some effort into making it happen. You can block off time on your calendar – and I suggest varying the time of day. I use my Apple watch as a trigger. After I've been sitting too long, my watch reminds me to *stand up!* I take that as my cue to get up and take a MBWA lap around the workplace.
- **Do it alone** – Don't bring anyone else with you. Remember that your intent is to build personal connections. That's best accomplished when you're alone. I think you'll find that you can have great conversations one-on-one, or even one-on-two or one-on-more – as long as you're the *one*. Your team members will likely be less intimidated and more likely to speak up if you're alone.
- **Don't just visit with your "friends"** – It's easy to talk with the extroverts, those individuals who are just bursting with energy, but it's important to make an effort to engage with *all* of your employees, especially the introverts who are less likely to speak up on their own.
- **Ask for input** – Don't be afraid to ask for opinion and perspective. I often ask: *What do you think about…?* Or, *What's on your mind today?* Or, *What's one thing you think we could do better?* I have found that those questions can be very powerful, not just to promote engagement, but to help me to understand what's really going on!

- **Don't get defensive. Let your people talk. Let your people vent if that's what they want/need to do** – I have to admit that I struggle with this one. Some of what I hear is critical of management, or other team members. I want to defend our people and policies and actions, but I remind myself that the whole point of these MBWA conversations is to encourage exactly this kind of input. Getting defensive tends to decrease the likelihood of anyone sharing their concerns/issues in the future.

Profit Sharing

Earlier in this chapter, I wrote about our profit-sharing program. I believe that the sharing of profit is the ultimate way to build connections with your employees. This is another policy my father, Helmut, implemented after he bought Olympus. It took him a couple of years to turn the company around, but right from the start, he made a commitment to his team members that he would share the company's success with them. They would get a piece of the action! He held true to his word and established a profit-sharing plan that we still use today, and there's no question that it's one of the most engaging benefits we offer.

Here's how we do it. We share 20% of our pre-tax profits with our employees, and we do it in a very egalitarian way – everyone gets the same amount! The formula is simple arithmetic: Total Pre-Tax Profit times 20%, divided by Total Number of Employees.

It's worth noting that many of our team members are also eligible for performance bonuses in addition to their share of the profits. That part is not as egalitarian, but it has also proven to be effective.

Strategic Plan

Going back to our Strategic Plan, we might include a program to address scrap waste, with a 1% reduction as our goal. That would translate that into a $100,000 cost savings over the course of a year. Another component might be a 10% efficiency improvement, which would create $300,000 in additional profit. Still another goal might be a .5% reduction in our Cost Of Goods Sold, which would drop $200,000 more to the bottom line.

Obviously, adding $600,000 in pre-tax profits would be good for Olympus, but what's the value of that accomplishment to the people doing most of the work? Where's the incentive for them to do the heavy lifting to make it happen? Our profit-sharing plan puts skin in the game for every employee. If we start a year with a goal of adding $600,000 to our bottom line, I can look every employee in the eye and tell them that achieving that goal will put an additional $500 in their pocket.

There's a movie called Office Space – something of a cult classic – which has a scene where an employee named Peter Gibbons is meeting with two consultants who have been hired to help the company downsize. They ask him about his motivation.

"The thing is," Peter says, "it's not that I'm lazy, it's that I just don't care. It's a problem of motivation, all right? If I work my butt off, and Initech ships a few extra units, I don't see another dime. So where's the motivation?"

I think it's fair to say that Peter is the exact opposite of *engaged*. But a profit-sharing plan could eliminate his lack of motivation. At Olympus, if we ship a few extra mascots and banners, the profit we make on those sales goes right into our profit sharing plan, and in turn, provides us with a tool to engage the Peter Gibbons' of the world.

We hand out our profit-sharing checks right before Christmas. It's my favorite day of the year because I get to play Santa Claus. I share a high-level overview of our results, and then I walk around and individually hand out the checks. I get to personally thank every single employee, and I've had numerous employees break into tears. I've had many others share personal stories about what they are going to do with the money:

"My daughter's quinceañerais is coming up. I am going to use this money to rent a house and throw her a party she will always remember."

"My kids have wanted an Xbox for years. Christmas is going to be so special for them this year."

This book is all about engagement. Sharing success with our team members has increased the levels of employee engagement at Olympus pretty significantly. And, man, is it fun to do!

Make it Personal

From *The Godfather*, by Mario Puzo: *"Don't let anybody kid you. It's all personal, every bit of business. They call it business, OK, but it's all personal as hell. You know where I learned that from? The Don. My old man. The Godfather."*

Yes, business is personal. You spend a third of your adult life at work, right? I know that I have become pretty good friends with some of my co-workers, not to mention some of our customers and some of our suppliers. I know that I truly care about them. To build those connections, you need to make it personal. If you want high levels of engagement, you have to connect, and to connect you have to take it beyond purely transactional.

Southwest Airlines is arguably the most successful transportation company in the United States over the last 20+ years. Southwest makes everything personal! Have you ever heard a Southwest gate agent or flight attendant make an announcement that sounded like they were reading from a memorized script? I flew on my birthday a few years ago, and one of the flight attendants presented me with a "birthday cake" made from toilet paper, cocktail sticks and cherries. It wasn't edible – or even attractive – but it was creative and funny, and most importantly, it made me feel special and appreciated. I shared photos of this creation with friends and family, and I still have it saved on my phone today.

I try to do the same thing at Olympus. As a company, we try to make it personal – and make it fun! – to show employees that we care. Here are a few of the things we do to help us connect:

- Birthday Cards for Kids – We send personal cards to our employees' kids on their birthdays, with a little bit of money enclosed. We've found this to be a touching way to connect with our employees' families.
- Graduations – Graduating from high school is a big achievement for many of our employees' families. We recognize all of our graduates and send them personal cards and gifts.
- Work Anniversaries and Birthdays – Every employee gets a *congratulations* message on their birthday, and a *thank you* on their work anniversary.
- Special Occasions – Babies, weddings, etc. These are the most important dates in someone's life. We send personalized gifts anytime one of our team-members gets married or has a baby.

- Employees In The News – We're always on the lookout for "news" that includes our team members. It might be formal (something in the newspaper) or informal (something we hear through the grapevine), but we're actively looking for news that then lets us recognize our employees' public accomplishments.
- Scholarship Program – We offer a scholarship program to the children and grandchildren of our employees.
- Fun Parties – We are intentional about planning off-site parties and picnics to help foster these connections.

There's no magic bullet in developing connections. It takes time and a conscious effort to get to know your team members. But this is an area where your Return On Investment potential is also very high. Dave wrote earlier that you have to have an *investment attitude* in order to be a successful marketer. I believe that the same sort of attitude will make you a more successful manager on the "people side" of your business. Everything from the birthday cards to the profit sharing program is an investment in our future at Olympus, and we're seeing a consistent payoff.

9 Measurement and Accountability
Dave Fellman

It didn't surprise me at all to read that Brian's Big Hairy Audacious Goal is to pay out $1 million in profit sharing to his team members. That's 100% consistent with Olympus' Mission Statement: *At Olympus, we want to create a rewarding work environment for our team.*

Beyond that, it's 100% consistent with all of the rest of his philosophy on employee engagement. *If I build the kind of company that the best people will want to work for, we'll all be successful.*

There's more to it than just being good to your employees, though. That's something Brian and I both agree on. They have to be good to you too! The "goodies" are all meant to support high levels of engagement, leading to high levels of performance. And that's a great segue into one of my favorite topics, putting *measurement* into *management*.

Measurement is critical. Why? First of all, so you'll know how you're doing! But of equal importance, so you'll know how *everyone else* is doing in terms of helping you to reach your overall goals.

Measurement is the foundation of accountability. As Louis V. Gerstner, Jr., the former CEO of IBM, has said: "People don't do what you expect, but what you inspect." (That's one of Brian's favorite quotes!)

It Starts With Goals

Let's continue the conversation about measurement and accountability by arranging a few pieces on a board. You have goals, right? (If you don't, we have a fundamental problem!) But whether you do or you don't, let's consider the reason(s) that you *should have* goals. I think there are three reasons:

1. To provide a destination
2. To provide a scale of measurement
3. To provide motivation

The most common definition of "destination" refers to a place; for example, *the place designated as the end of a journey*. An alternate definition states that "destination" can also refer to *the ultimate goal for which something is done*. To further explain, vocabulary.com used these words: "The state of affairs that a plan is intended to achieve and that (when achieved) terminates behavior intended to achieve it."

Let me digress for just a moment. *The ultimate goal for which something is done* is useful to my story. *The state of affairs, etc.* sounds like someone trying to sound smarter than everyone else. This is a book about *engagement*, which is a function of *communication*, which as we've noted, requires that everyone can connect the dots. *Jargon* is sometimes useful, but often it's the enemy of communication. What my Dad used to call "stilted" language is sometimes necessary, but more often, it's the enemy of communication *and* engagement. Have you ever been turned off by someone who seemed to be more interested in showing off their huge vocabulary than by actually communicating with you? Let's not do that when it's our turn to talk!

Back to "destination." I want you to have goals so you'll know what you're hoping to achieve.

Scale of Measurement

I want you to have a *scale of measurement* so you'll know when you get there! Let's relate this to the science of *navigation*, which is the process of getting from one place to another. Again, *process* is a key word. In order to navigate successfully, the process requires that you know your starting point and your end point – your destination! It helps, too, if you can identify and avoid known hazards, and anticipate unforeseen hazards. It's also beneficial to have time-and-distance benchmarks, so you can know if you're on schedule.

I used to be a pilot. (Actually, I'm still a pilot, but I used to be much more active.) I learned to fly just as GPS was coming available to private pilots.

GPS was great, because it let us navigate "direct" from starting point to destination. Before GPS, we used radio-based "navaids" called VOR's and NDB's.

Using these navaids was actually much like using GPS on the roads today. In a car, your GPS might take you north on an Interstate, then west on a state road, then northwest on a city street to get to your destination. In a plane, you might track inbound to the VOR from the south, then track outbound at a specific compass heading toward the next waypoint. This could get more complex as you got close to your destination. For example, my home field, which had no navaids or control tower of its own, was in-between VOR's, about 20 miles south of one and 25 miles northwest of another. If I was coming in from the south, I first navigated to the VOR, watching a set of needles on a dial until they told me I was overhead the radio beacon, then I followed the radio signal outbound on a heading of 285 degrees. My airplane flew at 150 mph, so 10 minutes of flying time should put me right over the field.

Headwinds or tailwinds could make it a little more complicated than that, but not prohibitively. Of greater concern was an "antenna farm" that included three radio/TV broadcast towers, one of which extended more than 1800 feet into the air. These towers were located 8 miles from the VOR, on the same 285 degree radial. To avoid that "known hazard," I would stay above 2000 feet for 5 minutes after turning outbound at the VOR. Basic old-fashioned, time/speed/distance navigation!

Here's some more of that. Let's say, for the sake of discussion, that the distance from my starting point to the VOR was 150 miles, on a straight line. As noted, my airplane flew at 150 mph. (It could go faster, but 150 was its most fuel-efficient cruising speed.) At normal cruise, that leg should take exactly one hour.

What would it mean if it took 65 minutes? A headwind! By the same token, if it took only 55 minutes, that meant I had a tailwind. Maybe I should clarify that 150 mph is the speed at which my airplane could travel through the air. The air itself is usually moving. That's what wind is! Flying at an airspeed of 150 mph into a headwind of 10 mph yields a groundspeed of 140 mph, and you're behind schedule. An airspeed of 150 mph plus a tailwind of 10 mph yields a groundspeed of 160 mph, putting you ahead of schedule. I could also go on about true wind and apparent wind and wind vectors here, but I don't want to sound like that guy who's trying to sound smarter than everyone else. The point is that all of this can be measured!

So first you establish your destination, then you plot your course – avoiding the known hazards and hopefully anticipating anything else that might go wrong. Then you follow your course, hopefully reaching your goal, on plan and on schedule. If you're off schedule – ahead or behind – it's good to know that, right? And the more thought you give to those unforeseen hazards, the better prepared you stand to be if something does go wrong.

Motivation

The third part of the "goals equation" is motivation. In 1968, Edwin A. Locke published a groundbreaking study called *Toward a Theory of Task Motivation and Incentive*. In it, he demonstrated that employees are motivated by clear, well-defined goals and feedback.

For the purposes of our discussion, I want you to consider yourself an employee as well. Which is true, right? You may be "Employee #1," but you are still, in one form or another, one of your company's *human resources*. The *human* part of that suggests that you might need motivation too!

Locke's study suggested 5 principles of effective goalsetting:

1. Clarity. A goal must be specific and clear.
2. Challenge. An easy or tedious goal is demotivating. But keep a realistic balance: don't expect anyone on your team to spin straw into gold.
3. Commitment. Your employees have to understand and buy in to the goal from the outset.
4. Feedback. Provide regular feedback throughout the whole process. This helps to keep the goal on track.
5. Task complexity. Think about realistic timescales, and break down the process into sub-goals with regular reviews.

George T. Doran published a paper in the November 1981 issue of *Management Review* that extended upon Locke's findings. It was titled: "There's A S.M.A.R.T. Way To Write Management's Goals And

Objectives". As you might have guessed, this was the genesis of the SMART Goals philosophy, which states that goals must be:

- Specific
- Measurable
- Achievable
- Relevant
- Time-bound

Locke and Doran were fundamentally in agreement, with maybe a little bit different emphasis on certain points. What I take from Locke is the emphasis on *feedback*, and from Doran, the importance of *relevance*.

It's worth mentioning, I think, that some people express the R in the SMART acronym as "Reasonable." In fact, I've heard it said that you only need 2 principles for effective goalsetting, *reasonable* and *measurable*. To me, *reasonable* and a*chievable* are essentially the same, so SMART covers that. *Relevant* is something different. On one hand, it's a means of separating *important* from *trivial*. More importantly, though, is the element of being *relevant/important* to each individual you're hoping to motivate. Here's a rule of thumb: *The bigger your organization, and the more diverse each individual's responsibilities, the more you have to be concerned with* individual *relevance.*

One Example

That's true of small organizations with diverse responsibilities as well. One of my clients established a quality goal, with a mission statement to support it. The goal was to achieve 100% customer satisfaction with the quality of the product over a 30 day period. The mission statement was: *We won't let it out the door unless we're all 100% sure it will meet or exceed our customer's expectations.*

My client held a staff meeting to kick off this program. He went from individual to individual to explain each person's role in achieving the goal. The salesperson was responsible for understanding and communicating the customer's expectations. The two craftsmen were responsible for fabricating the product, following every quality control step along the way. The owner himself was responsible for the final quality inspection, and the installer was responsible for making sure that nothing was damaged or went wrong with the install. Then the salesperson was responsible for making sure that the customer was, in fact, completely satisfied with the quality. Then the bookkeeper was responsible for making sure that the invoice was correct.

Over the first 30 days, this program was a complete success. On Day 31, the owner held another staff meeting, the theme of which was: *"Congratulations, thank you, and let's do it again."* Over 10 months, they have achieved their goal 9 times, and the month they missed, the theme of the staff meeting was: *"OK, we weren't perfect this month, but we know that we can be. Let's just refocus on our goal!"*

It's worth mentioning, I think, that there was no tangible incentive attached to this goal in the beginning – in other words, no cash or special privileges. After three consecutive months of achievement, the staff meeting featured a catered lunch. For each month after that, including the month they missed, everyone got something extra, ranging from gift cards to driving privileges in the owner's Jaguar. The key point, of course, is that the goal itself motivated these people to achieve it. Locke and Doran were right!

Straw Into Gold

Locke also had something interesting to say about *reasonable/achievable* — that the best way to feel motivated is to push yourself to do something that you're not 100% certain you can achieve. According to Locke, a little workplace challenge is not a bad thing. Tackling challenging goals headfirst allows an individual to work hard, develop his/her skills, and reap the rewards in terms of positive feedback and a sense of personal achievement.

I tend to agree, but with one caveat. If you ask me to "spin straw into gold' – Locke's own words for setting the bar especially high – you can't punish me for failing to reach what you knew from the start was a very ambitious target. If, however, the goal was fully reasonable and achievable, there have to be consequences for not achieving it. That's what accountability is all about.

Whether that takes the form of *punishment* depends on the situation. You could make the case, I guess, that any negative consequence is a punishment, but obviously some things are more punishing than others. For example, I'm not sure I'd call an "attitude adjustment" a punishment – and believe me, I've had my attitude adjusted a few times! But if an attitude adjustment doesn't take hold, the next stage has to hurt more. That could range from loss of privilege to loss of income to loss of job! More on that to follow.

****

You may be "Employee #1," but you are still, in one form or another, one of your company's human resources.

When I wrote that sentence, I was reminded of my first "real" job, at Chase Shawmut Company. Granted, it was a summer job, but it was the first time I had worked at a real company. Before that, I'd earned money by mowing lawns and shoveling snow. The closest thing I'd had to a real job was working as an umpire for the local Little League.

The reason I'm mentioning this is that I was interviewed and hired at Chase Shawmut by a department called "Personnel Management." And I remember, during my sweeper days, that every once in a while, the PA system would announce that someone was "wanted in Personnel."

According to an *HR Magazine* article that I found online, the first Personnel Management department started at the National Cash Register Company in 1900. John Henry Patterson, NCR's founder, organized this department to deal with grievances, discharges, safety and training after several strikes and employee lockouts had occurred. To put that another way, he organized the department in order to *engage* more effectively with his employees.

The terminology related to all of this started to change in the late 1950's, and the first use of the term "human resources" in its modern form was in a 1958 report by an economist named E. Wight Bakke. Before too long, *Personnel* went the way of the dinosaur and *HR* became the standard nomenclature.

Now, I'm imaging a scene in some company conference room, or an executive's office, circa 1968. Someone has raised the issue of changing the department name. "Why?" asks the most senior manager. "To show them we care about them," is the answer. "'Personnel' says to me that they work *for* us. I want 'Human Resources' to communicate that they work *with* us."

"I like the idea," the senior manager says, "but let's try to make this clear. It's not just that we care about them, it's that we *value* them."

Not sayin' it ever happened this way. But if it had, it would have happened for exactly the right reason. I think, too often, companies follow the current trend without thinking too much about it. The American Society for Personnel Administration was founded in 1948. At some point, it changed its name to the Society for Human Resource Management. I can also imagine a let's-change-the-name conversation in which a senior manager asked *why*, and was told: "Because that's what everyone is calling it now." On one hand, I guess it's a positive to be in step with the times. But on the other hand, changing the name of a department won't all by itself increase engagement.

Imagine this scene, though: The President and other Senior Managers, including the newly named Director of Human Resources, addressing the rest of the company's employees.

"We're changing the name of our Personnel Department, to Human Resources. This is something that many companies are doing, but we're not doing it just to be copycats. We're hoping to communicate that we look at you, not just as *personnel* who work for us, but as *resources* who contribute. And we're hoping to communicate that we value you, and your contribution to our success. Can we do this by just using different words? Of course not! But we want you to view this as a starting point, and *engage* with us toward better communication all around."

****

Measurement Strategy

Goals must be measurable. Let's take that a step further and say that *performance* must be measurable. Sometimes that's easy, sometimes not so much.

As noted, Brian and I met in October 2018, when we spoke on the same program at the SGIA Expo. We spoke briefly before the program started, then at length afterward when we realized that we might have some synergy. The initial conversation, as I recall, was mostly about his Brewers and my Red Sox, both of whom were competing in their Division Series. We decided that a Brewers-Red Sox World Series would be a lot of fun.

It didn't turn out that way, but I was happy enough with the Sox beating the Dodgers, in perhaps the most measurable endeavor known to man. Think about baseball for just a minute. Each pitch is either a ball or a strike, and you count 'em up. Each at-bat is either a success or a failure – safely on base or out – and that can be measured too. Sometimes an out is an immediate and irrevocable failure. Sometimes an out is a complete and total success; for example, a sacrifice fly that drives in the winning run. Each game results in a win or a loss, and the teams with the most wins keep moving forward, through the regular season, then the playoffs, and eventually the winner of the last game of each season is crowned the World Series Champion.

Individual performance is measured too. Batting average, runs-batted-in and home runs are the "Triple Crown" measurements for batters. Wins vs. losses, strikeout percentage and innings pitched are among the most important statistics for pitchers. Put-outs, assists and errors are counted for fielders. As more and more data is collected and collated, modern teams have metrics for just about everything. Wanna know how well Mookie Betts performed in July 2018 against left-handed pitchers throwing split-finger fastballs? I'm sure the Red Sox could tell you!

That kind of measurement is easy, because it's all pretty simple arithmetic. The *interpretation* is often more complex, but I'll get to that in a minute. The important point here is that numerical/statistical goals provide you with a very black-and-white picture of whether a goal was achieved, or not.

Let's say that Mookie started the 2018 season with a goal of hitting 30 home runs. He hit number 30 in the next to last game of the regular season. Goal achieved! He hit another one in the same game. Goal exceeded! He hit one more in the last game of the regular season, to finish with 32, or 107% of his goal.

Interpretation

What if his goal had been 35 home runs? Obviously he would have failed to achieve that goal. But here's where the interpretation comes in. Mookie played in 136 of the team's 162 regular season games, so he averaged one home run for each 4.25 games. If he'd played in all 162 games and maintained the same average, he would have finished with 38 homers. Goal exceeded!

But wait, almost no one plays in all 162 games. In fact, only 6 Major Leaguers did it in 2018, and that number has been pretty consistent over the last 10-15 years. With 30 Major League teams, each carrying 25 players on their roster for each game, that's 6 out of 750, or 8 tenths of one percent. (If you want to get technical, Major League teams are allowed to expand their rosters for the last month of each season, so the number of players is actually greater than 750, but that just lowers the *percentage* of 162-gamers. It's still a very rare occurrence.)

Since playing in all 162 games is unlikely, Mookie's goalsetting process should have considered that in the first place. Maybe the goal could have been to play in 150 games and hit 30 home runs. In that case, he would have failed to reach the first goal, but still achieved the second one. As a Red Sox fan, I would probably have been happy with that.

Hierarchy of Goals

Actually, I was completely happy with that, because the Red Sox won the 2018 World Series even with Mookie missing 36 games. And that brings me to the main point I'm hoping to make here. The best goalsetting involves a *hierarchy* of goals, or to put that differently, one *main goal* supported by a number of *component goals*. I'm pretty sure that Mookie's Main Goal for 2018 was to win the World Series. From that point, he could ask himself: *What do I have to do in order to support that goal?* Playing in 150 games and hitting 30 home runs could have been component goals. *Improving my performance against left-handed pitchers throwing split-finger fastballs* could have been another one.

These are all things that can be measured. I'm going to make up some numbers now and say that Mookie hit .225 against those split-finger lefties in 2017. His *improving my performance* goal was to hit .275 against them in

2018. It's not unreasonable to think that the "extra" focus that goal provided would result in its achievement. But let's paint a different picture. Let's say that 50 games into the year, Mookie was still hitting .225 against split-finger lefties. If you'll accept that the primary reason for goalsetting is connected to motivation, this is where the secondary reason comes into play. *What I'm doing isn't working! If I continue just doing what I've been doing, my goal is in jeopardy. Wake-up call!*

On the other side of that coin, at some point, it became apparent that Mookie would not play in 150 games in 2018. But if the team was still performing at World Series level, and if he was ahead of or at least on track with most of the rest of his component goals, the games-played goal would probably not sink to the level of *de-motivator*. Because, in the hierarchy of goals, it was simply not as important as the Main Goal. *Part of*, and possibly *critical to*, but possibly not. But definitely one of the things that could be/ should be measured on the path to the ultimate destination.

Management Perspective

Now let's take a different perspective on the goalsetting process. How would you like to be the GM of the Red Sox for a little while? Your Main Goal is to win the World Series next season. Your immediate challenge is to work backwards from that goal to establish your component goals.

You might start by saying: *"I think 95 wins will get us into the playoffs."* (In 2018, the lowest ranked team in the playoffs won 91 games in the regular season.) *"What do I need from each of my starting pitchers to achieve 95 wins?"* (Starts, wins, innings pitched, plus any other relevant metric.) *"What do I need from my hitters to achieve 95 wins?"* (At bats, hits, runs, runs-batted-in, plus any other relevant metric.) *"What do I need from my fielders to achieve 95 wins?"* (Put outs, assists, plus, again, any other relevant metric.) *"What do I need from my manager? My coaches? My medical staff? My office staff? My marketing team?"*

This is *comprehensive* goalsetting, and it's the same process, whether you're talking about a baseball team or any other organization. And, as you're setting these goals, keep Locke and Doran in mind. Whether you use SMART or any other acronym, this is all about *destination* and *measurement*, with *motivation* as the principal outcome.

Subjective Measurement

So far, I've been talking about *objective* measurement. According to the Online Business Dictionary (businessdictionary.com), *objective* refers to the elimination of subjective perspectives and a process that is purely based on hard facts. *Subjective* measurement, on the other hand, refers to personal perspectives, feelings, or opinions entering the decision-making process.

I noted earlier that there's room for interpretation in most statistical analysis, but that's not what I'm talking about now. *Subjective* measurement is not fact-based, but it's handy in situations where facts aren't fully present.

Here's an example. Fred is a salesperson. His Main Goal for last year was $1,000,000 in sales. He didn't achieve it. He finished the year at $785,000.

OK, why did he fail to reach his goal? One *fact* that's available is that he lost a major customer mid-way through the year. That customer spent $100,000 the previous year and was on track to spend about the same until they stopped placing orders in August. Their total for the year was $58,000, so now we have an explanation for about a quarter of Fred's shortfall.

Here's another *fact* that's available. Fred's year-before-last total was $850,000. The goalsetting process for last year was based on gaining $50,000 in business from his current customers and finding $100,000 worth of new customers. He only gained $50,000 worth of new customers, so now we know where about another quarter of his shortfall came from. A customer-by-customer analysis would tell us exactly where the rest of the shortfall came from, but here's the big question: Would it tell us *why?*

In some cases, it probably would. Let's say that the major customer referenced earlier went out of business. Hard to blame Fred for that! But on the other hand, let's say that they just stopped placing orders, and no one knows exactly why. (Does that sound familiar? If so, it points to a need for a much greater level of *customer engagement.* More on *that* to follow.) Here's another possibility. Let's say that there were quality problems, which Fred was unable to resolve. The first scenario has an *objective* explanation. The latter two represent a *subjective* opportunity.

Skills and Attitudes

I have long believed that success comes from a combination of skills and attitudes. A few years ago, I started applying that to my consulting work by adding a subjective evaluation and purely subjective goals to the goalsetting process. As noted, I do a lot of work with printing companies, and here is a list of skills and attitudes I developed to evaluate printing salespeople

1. General knowledge of printing processes
2. Specific knowledge of the company's capabilities
3. Ability to "work the program"
4. Willingness to "work the program"
5. Understanding of the company's value proposition
6. Ability to present the company's value proposition
7. Questioning skills
8. Listening skills
9. Team skills and attitudes
10. Reporting and recordkeeping skills and attitudes

Some of this probably requires explanation. Numbers 1 and 2 are different in that it's one thing to know how the ink gets on the paper, it's another thing to understand exactly what your company is capable of doing, and where you're most likely to be competitive. Brian's company, for example, is in a niche where perhaps 5% of the 35,000-or-so printing companies in the United States can play. The other side of that coin, though, is that Olympus Group is simply not well-equipped for other types of printing. If you need a custom-printed theatrical stage curtain, Brian's your guy. If you need 250 business cards, or 250,000 catalogs, he is not. Unfortunately, industry-wide, we have far too many salespeople who chase orders which are out of their niche.

Numbers 3 and 4 refer to the ability and the willingness – two different things, right? – to follow an overall sales strategy. For example:

1 Identify a likely suspect company
2 Identify the decision-maker
3 Send an introductory communication
4 Follow up on that introductory communication
5 Deal with predictable early-stages obstacles and objections
6 Schedule and conduct a needs/wants analysis
7 Use the results of that analysis to qualify or disqualify

8 If qualified, prepare and present a customized proposal

9 Deal with predictable later-stages obstacles and objections

10 Close the sale

11 Perform whatever role the salesperson is supposed to perform in terms of production, installation, etc.

12 Schedule and conduct a "post-mortem" to ensure customer satisfaction

13 Identify another likely suspect company and do it all again

This probably seems pretty basic. All salespeople do this stuff, right? Sadly, many do not. We have lots of underachievers in sales, and that's not just in the printing industry.

Value Proposition

Numbers 5 and 6 refer to the understanding and ability to present the company's value proposition – again, understanding and ability are two different things, just like ability and willingness. And importantly, I'm not talking about the company's Core Values here, which Brian discussed earlier. This is about the value *the customer* derives from doing business with you.

I want to say two things here. First, don't ever forget that value is ultimately determined by the buyer, not the seller. The seller can say: *"We think this represents value."* The buyer has to agree before that statement becomes truth. Beauty, they say, is in the eye of the beholder. Value is too.

The second thing is my own personal definition of a value proposition. I found this definition on investopedia.com: *A value proposition refers to the value a company promises to deliver to customers should they choose to buy their product.* My own definition is a function of where this tends to apply to the real world – when a seller is faced with a price objection. Here's my definition of value proposition: *The reason(s) why my product is worth more than the other seller's product.*

I shared my observation earlier that most people will spend what they have to spend in order to get what they want, or what they need. Often, that requires a salesperson to explain a value proposition!

A salesperson who can't – or won't – do that is unlikely to be a top achiever.

Evaluation Process

Numbers 7 through 10 refer to other important skills – all representing factors that might be holding a salesperson back from reaching objective goals. This is not meant to be *the* definitive list, by the way, but I hope you'll agree that it's at least a starting point for your own subjective evaluation list. Now we come to the active stage of this process.

On a scale of 1-10, how would you rate (Salesperson) in terms of general knowledge of printing processes?

On the same scale of 1-10, how would you rate (Salesperson) in terms of specific knowledge of the company's capabilities?

You see where I'm going with this, right? It's the same question, times each of the skills and attitudes on your list. Your purely subjective 1-10 ratings give you a starting point, from which you can establish an improvement goal, and an improvement plan.

Overall Rating

Before I go deeper into that, here's a little wrinkle I've developed recently. I now start the process by asking my client to give me an overall rating: *On a scale of 1-10, how would you rate (Salesperson)'s overall performance?* Or a variation on that theme: *On a scale of 1-10, how would you rate your satisfaction with (Salesperson)'s overall performance?*

Next, we do the individual factor assessments, which I summarize on a spreadsheet, adding the one number which almost always tends to be the biggest eye-opener. That number is that average of all the individual factor assessments, and it is almost always lower than the overall assessment. For example: *In terms of overall performance, I give (Salesperson) an 8.* Then the average of the individual factors comes out to 6.6! That would open your eyes, wouldn't it?

Improvement Goal and Plan

Once you know what's holding an individual back, you can start working on improvement, and that takes us back to Locke and Doran. It should also take us to what I suspect is one of your own greatest improvement issues – *time management!* Because here I am, getting ready to suggest that you add something else to your already busy days.

The key to time management is to prioritize. If you don't have time to do everything, do at least the most important things!

So let's say that (Salesperson) rates three 8's, three 7's, two 6's and two 4's against my list of ten critical skills and attitudes. Let's also say that you realistically have enough time (and possibly other resources) to address two of those. On the surface, it may seem like the 4's are the areas most in need of attention, but that may not be true. Let's make one of the 4's *team skills and attitudes*, and the other one *reporting and recordkeeping skills and attitudes*. Now, let's make the 6's *listening skills* and *specific knowledge of the company's capabilities*.

Yes, I would like (Salesperson) to be a better teammate, but is that as important as listening skills in terms of reaching the Main Goal? Is recordkeeping as important as knowing what the hell we sell? If you don't have time to do everything, do at least the most important things!

Now, let's talk about rest of the goals equation, combining Locke and Doran:

- Specific
- Measurable
- Achievable
- Relevant
- Time-bound
- Clarity
- Challenge
- Commitment
- Feedback
- Task complexity

You probably can't snap your fingers and turn (Salesperson) from a 6 to a 10 in any category. So how about this as a component goal: *Over the next 30 days, we will focus on your listening skills with the goal of getting you from a 6 to a 7. Over the next 30 days after that, we will continue to focus on your listening skills with the goal of getting you from a 7 to an 8. Then we'll consider what to work on next!*

Now, let's not forget that these are purely subjective ratings. There's no universal scale for listening skills, this is you saying: *"I think you're a 6, and my goal is to get you to an 8."*

Clarity requires you to take a further step: *"Let me tell you why I rated you at 6, and let me tell you what I think 7 looks like, and 8."*

Relevant also requires another step: *"Let me tell you how I think all of this will help you."*

Feedback requires that you provide, well, feedback. On a regular basis! *"Let's meet every Monday to talk specifically about this. I'll tell you how I think you're doing. You tell me what challenges you're facing. We'll work together to reach this goal."*

I have another term to describe all of this: *Employee engagement!*

By the way, are you wondering exactly how to go about improving someone's listening skills? Here's what I did. I went to Google and searched on *"How do you improve someone's listening skills?"* I found links to a number of articles written by and for elementary school teachers, who are on the front lines of this issue every day. I found nothing that was "snap-your-fingers" simple, but a lot that was helpful.

One more thought on the Improvement Plan. Based on your situation and priorities, you might go 30-60-90 days on a single issue, or work at one thing for some number of days and then move on to another thing. Again, it's all about priorities, and getting the best return on your investment of time and other resources.

Non-Sales Employees

I have also developed a starting-point list for subjective evaluation of non-sales employees:

1. Job Skills
2. Initiative
3. Dedication to the Company
4. Dedication to the Team
5. Work Ethic
6. "Like Factor"
7. "Trust Factor"

8. Potential For Advancement
9. Communication Skills — Verbal
10. Communication Skills — Listening

As with the sales list, some of it may require explanation. I draw a distinction between *dedication to the company* and *dedication to the team*. The distinction is really between dedication to owners and managers and dedication to co-workers. The *like factor* is all about whether people like the individual. The *trust factor* is a deeper issue, wouldn't you agree? And it's worth mentioning, I think, that several of my clients have been much more specific about job skills. One, in fact, the owner of a catering company, expanded the list to include six specific job skills and attitudes, ranging from recipe skills to knife skills to a "cleanliness attitude."

Reward vs. Punishment

Now we come to the *accountability* part of the conversation. As I wrote earlier, *measurement is the foundation of accountability*. And as Brian wrote earlier: *Measurement. Feedback. Accountability. When these come together in the right way, they are powerful motivators.* So what does it mean for them to come together in the right way?

First come the goals. Then comes the measurement. Then comes the feedback. *Positive* feedback is the first stage of *reward*. *Negative* feedback is the first stage of *punishment*. Both can be motivators all by themselves, and that's pretty obvious on the positive side. Brian has written pretty extensively about the power of "pats on the back." But negative feedback can also be a positive motivator. Do you remember my story about the shop foreman at Chase Shawmut Company?

> *People told me that he could be every bit as scary as he looked. "You don't want to be on his bad side," I was told. But I was also told: "You don't want to let him down." Even as a college-age kid, I understood the difference between those two feelings. People didn't want to let him down because they respected him, not just because there was some reason to fear him.*

Earlier, I told you about the day he patted me on the back. Now, I have to tell you about the day he caught me taking a late-morning, hangover nap in the shed where we kept the lawnmower and some other outside maintenance tools. I didn't hear him come in. All of a sudden, I was wide awake and there he was, head shaking from side to side. He spoke just four words – "I'm disappointed in you" – and then he walked out of the shed.

This was maybe two weeks before I went back to school. I don't remember if he spoke to me during those two weeks. I do remember that he wished me well on my last day and told me that I'd be welcome back next summer. I'm pretty sure that's because he saw me working extra hard over those last two weeks – a pattern of behavior motivated by his handling of my mistake. He would have been justified in enacting some serious punishment. I'm not sure he wouldn't have been justified in firing me on the spot! But instead, he turned the negative into a positive.

"I'm disappointed in you" can be a very powerful and positive motivator, but that requires certain conditions to pre-exist, the first of which is an *engaged* employee, who understands what is expected, both in terms of performance and attitude. I look back on the nap incident and realize that I was the recipient of the most gentle form of "attitude adjustment." As I've noted, I've had my attitude adjusted more than once, and it was usually far less gentle!

Correction vs. Punishment

We might think of attitude adjustment as the Plan A for accountability, and this is true whether we're talking about a skills issue or an attitude issue. Let's say that one of Brian's sewers makes a technical mistake. The *correction* for that mistake might suggest further training, but it also might be just one of those things. (As I wrote earlier, Murphy's Law is very real in a business like Brian's!) If it is just one of those things, the correction/attitude adjustment might range from "I'm disappointed in you" to "This is not OK!"

But what if that doesn't resolve the issue? What if the same mistake keeps being made, or the same bad attitude displayed? Now we have to consider *punishment*, which could range from loss of privilege to loss of income to loss of job!

There's no one-size-fits-all solution to this sort of problem, but there are two things I want you to think about. First, while goals and expectations must be *reasonable* and *measurable*, punishment must be *reasonable* and *fair*. If it's not reasonable, or fair to the employee involved, you might find yourself in legal trouble. And beyond that, it must seem reasonable and fair to the rest of your team, because there's always the element of *I could be next!*

Second, there's another consideration regarding the rest of your team. Consider this, your people – especially your superstars – know who's doing things right, and who's not. They know who's holding up their end, and who's dragging the team down. To put it simply, they know who's *engaged* and who's not, and they expect you to know too! More importantly, they expect you to apply *correction* and/or *punishment* any time it's required. If you don't – if you tolerate bad performance or bad behavior – you lose some of the credibility that's so important to your side of the engagement equation.

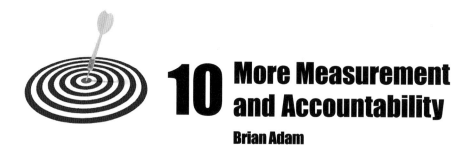

10 More Measurement and Accountability

Brian Adam

I have to admit that I found it painful to read the last chapter. Right at the beginning, Dave listed three reasons for developing and maintaining a solid goalsetting program:

1. To provide a destination
2. To provide a scale of measurement
3. To provide motivation

OK, no problem with any of that, but at Olympus, we have tried numerous times, and in numerous ways, to create effective goals for our team members. We have tried and failed, numerous times, and in numerous ways. But we have learned from our mistakes, and I invite you to learn from them too.

Mistake #1 – Too Many Goals

Going all the way back to 2005, our goalsetting process read something like this:

- Please create 3-5 personal development goals
- Please create 3-5 departmental goals
- Please think about 2-3 skills you'd like to improve

Let's think about this process for just a minute, using a salesperson as an example. Here's the actual goal set we received from a member of our sales team:

1. Complete 25 outbound sales calls to new prospects every week
2. Meet face-to-face with 2 current customers every week
3. Present to 5 new prospects every month
4. Attend 2 networking events every month
5. Identify 10 new high potential prospects every month
6. Spend 15 minutes each day reviewing orders with inside sales team partner
7. Attend 4 hours of instruction/training on Microsoft Excel
8. Join a local Toastmasters group to improve public speaking skills
9. Become an expert in a new print process which was recently introduced
10. Gain a better understanding of the new trends happening in the 3D printing space
11. Improve team use of the ERP system
12. Run a series of lunch-and-learns on the topic of *organization* to share knowledge with team members

Wow! Way too many goals, right? How would anyone be able to focus with such an exhaustive list of goals? Imagine that salesperson's weekly one-on-one meeting with his or her manager:

"So how are you doing against your annual goals"

"Glad you asked boss! I made 20 outbound calls last week, met with no current customers, and presented to one new prospect. I attended a networking event – hey, does a bowling league with my buddies count? In that case, it would be two. And I, well, I forgot the rest. What else did we have written down?"

What we learned was that these goals were not driving behavior. At best, our salesperson was taking actions, and then just reporting back, hoping that the actions would result in attainment of the goals. It wasn't working. But what exactly was missing?

Bill Gates and Warren Buffet have both been asked if they have any one-word explanation for what has made them so successful in business. They both answered with the same one word:

"FOCUS!"

Working too many goals is the exact opposite of *focused*. Our salesperson definitely operated with a lack of *focus*, but whose fault was that? At the very least, our goalsetting process contributed to the problem. If I ask you to work on twelve things at the same time, I'm probably setting you up to fail.

From this mistake, we learned to limit the number of goals for each team member. One goal is ideal for maximum focus, two goals is definitely manageable, but the rule at Olympus now is three goals max. Anything beyond three goals becomes too much to handle and makes focus impossible.

Mistake #2 – Too Long A Timeframe

For many years, we also followed the traditional process of *annual* goal setting. *"What are your goals for the upcoming year?"* To address Mistake #1, we limited the process. We asked every team member to commit to one and only one annual goal. *"What is the most important thing for you to accomplish this year?"* We then posted every team member's goal in the lunchroom, on one big board.

I thought this was a great idea – simple, transparent and it created some accountability, because everyone had to check off publicly when their goal was complete. Our published list of goals looked something like this:

Name	Goal	Completed
Brian Adam	Publish a book by the end of 2020	X
Dave Fellman	3 speaking engagements per month = Total of 36	X

We liked the simplicity, and everyone was on board, but you probably can guess what happened. Almost none of the goals were completed before November and December. Most of our team members would procrastinate throughout the year (myself included), and then we'd try to cram everything into the last two or three months. We learned that a year was too long for most of the goals we created!

It was later pointed out to me that we fell victim to Parkinson's Law, which states that "work expands so as to fill the time available for its completion." In other words, people usually take all the time allotted (and frequently more) to accomplish any task. That turns out to be especially true of goalsetting and achievement.

In 2016, we found what feels like the ideal solution to Mistake #2. As I noted earlier we implemented EOS (Entrepreneur's Operating System) from Gino Wickman's book *Traction*. EOS shares the belief that a year is too long and sets 90-day goals – "Rocks" in EOS terminology.

We have switched to a 90-day goal setting process and I LOVE IT! Our goals are more relevant, we review them more frequently, and we find that we're setting goals that are more easily attainable – given the *focus* that comes with something that must be completed in 90 days, as opposed to *allowing it* 365 days. We now have a much higher goal achievement rate.

And our goalsetting addresses more issues! In effect, we're all achieving four goals each year, not just one, but since it's only one goal at a time, it's not at the expense of *focus*.

Here's another benefit we've gained from EOS. Think about where you were 6 or 8 or 10 months ago. It's probably safe to assume that your focus has changed. Ours certainly did in 2020. Covid changed everything! But even looking back at 2019, we started that year too with a plan for our 1st through 4th Quarter Rocks. My own personal goal set was to focus on A, then B, then C and then D. By the time we got to the 3rd Quarter, though, it was apparent that D should be moved up over C, and by the beginning of the 4th Quarter, there was an E opportunity that hadn't even been on the radar at the beginning of the year.

On one hand, it's important to commit to your original goals. On the other hand, flexibility is important as well.

By the way, did you notice the difference between my goal and Dave's goal in the example above? Mine, to get this book published in 2020, was a perfect candidate for procrastination and Parkinson's Law. Dave's goal of 3 speaking engagements per month, adding up to 36 for the year, has built-in benchmarks. As Dave noted, goals must be *reasonable* and *measurable*.

Mistake #3 – Focusing on Weaknesses

Dave also spoke to the importance of prioritization in goalsetting in the previous chapter. In one example, he asked you to consider whether *team skills and attitudes* and *recordkeeping skills and attitudes* are as important as *listening skills* and *specific knowledge of the company's capabilities* to the performance of a salesperson. The point was to encourage us to focus on the attributes/skills that are most important to achieving our primary goals, not just the ones that define someone's weaknesses.

That was Mistake #3 for me. In one of the first performance reviews I created, I asked each individual to force-rank themselves against a list of attributes critical to their function. I wanted them to identify both their biggest strength and greatest weakness. I used the same sort of 1-10 scale Dave described earlier, but with one critical difference. Force-ranking meant they could only use each number once.

In other words, while Dave's system asks for a "how good" rating for each individual attribute, I asked for a rating *relative* to each attribute – this-is-my-best-thing, this-is-my-next-best-thing, and so on, all the way down to this-is-my-worst-thing.

What follows is an example of a salesperson's performance review:

Brian Adam Performance Review	
Attribute	**Ranking**
Listening Skills	7
Presentation Skills	1
Ability to Close	2
Prospecting	6
Product Knowledge	5
Record Keeping	9
EQ (emotional intelligence)	4
Team Skills	10
Persistence	8
Networking	3

After this self-evaluation, I took the two lowest scores (in this case Team Skills & Record Keeping) and we developed a performance improvement plan. We allocated precious time and resources towards improving these weaknesses. We got some results, BUT…

I'm in complete agreement with Dave. Our time would have been much better spent focused on other attributes that would have a greater impact on the greater goal – for a salesperson, that means driving sales volume. Had we focused on Listening Skills and Product Knowledge (even though these weren't the areas of greatest weakness), we would probably have produced *more meaningful* improvement.

Mistake #4 – Spend Too Much Time With Your Poorest Performers

When I first joined Olympus, we had about 14 members of the sales team. It was easy to identify the stars and the underperformers, and it seemed logical for me to dedicate and allocate most of my time to the latter group, the ones who were consistently missing their sales targets. We spent hours reviewing call lists, and polishing up sales pitches. I helped them develop prospect lists and joined them on sales calls. We'd meet frequently to track progress against the goals we'd set.

Meanwhile, I did little more than a monthly check-in with our top performers. Whatever they were doing was working, right? They were driving most of our volume, and I didn't want to get in their way.

Yup, Mistake #4! Now, many years later, I look back and think about those poor performers – whom I spent hours on end with, trying to develop them and improve their performance – with necessary emphasis on the words "look back" because they're no longer part of our team. The stars (at least most of them), are still here, and still driving a significant portion of our revenue.

What did I learn? While it's true that the stars don't need to be micromanaged, you can still have an impact by supporting them. By focusing on your stars, you can have an exponentially larger impact on your results. As Dave would say, you can use the same resources to turn a 5 into a 6 or a 7 into an 8. From 5 to 6, you have a little better underperformer. From 7 to 8, you go from *above-average* to *budding star*. And from 8 to 9 or 10, you go to *full-fledged star*.

Here's something else to consider. Real stars tend to have impact beyond their specific/primary responsibilities. Great salespeople, for example, tend to understand their customers really well. No, let me rephrase that, great salespeople tend to understand *your* customers really well, and with what they know about your customers and what they know about your internal operations, they can often identify internal areas of exposure, and roadblocks to the kind of sales growth and "happy customer" relationships we all want.

As an added bonus, if you're focused on your stars you can proactively address the risk of attrition. Here's a question you might ask each one of your top performers – and I might even suggest doing it tomorrow:

"Under what circumstances might you leave our company?"

There's real power in knowing the answer to that question for every one of your stars. At Olympus, we use this knowledge to make sure our superstars are fully engaged – and if they're not, we can probably do something about it before it's too late!

Regrettable Loses

One last thought related to poor performers and superstars. Many progressive companies track employee turnover and use it as a measure of employee engagement. I'm not a fan of this metric. I believe that some turnover within an organization is actually healthy.

If you lost your poorest performing salesperson, for example, and replaced that person by hiring a sales superstar away from a direct competitor, almost everyone would consider that a win. Yet in the traditional method of tracking turnover, it would be indistinguishable from any other loss.

At Olympus, we track turnover differently. We use a metric called "Regrettable Loss" – when an employee leaves, we simply ask their manager the following question:

"If (employee) reapplied for their current job, would you rehire them for this role?"

If they say "yes," we consider that a Regrettable Loss. If they say "no," we don't. We simply focus on hiring a replacement who will be an upgrade from the person we lost.

In a perfect world, you wouldn't have hired that poor performer in the first place – but I don't know anyone who operates in that perfect world. As hard as you try, there's always some margin for error in hiring another human to join your team. A high level of *engagement* improves your chances of a longer and more successful relationship than you might have had otherwise. And that's worth working towards, right? Especially with your stars and top performers and contributors.

****

Speaking of Top Contributors, that's a category that applies to your customers as well. Dave uses the term *Maximized Customer* to describe the ones who contribute the most to your business. For most companies, though – and certainly for Olympus – they're all not *maximized* yet. In the following two chapters, you'll learn how to get more value from more of your customers, and also what *value* means to them in the first place.

11 Customer Maximization

Dave Fellman

I've made numerous references to the four categories of people on the buying side of your selling equation: *suspects, prospects, customers* and *maximized customers*. I've promised several times that we'd get to Customer Maximization eventually, and here we are.

Here's the fundamental idea behind Customer Maximization. I believe that every current customer provides you with three levels of value. First is the value of *what they're buying from you now*. Second is the value of *what they could be buying from you*. Third is the value of *influence*; the ways in which current customers can help you to develop new customers.

Keep in mind that I'm not talking about the value you provide to them right now, or the value that you provide to your employees. We'll get to all of that in the following chapter!

First Level

What's most important about the First Level of Value – *the value of what they're buying from you now* – is that you protect it. After all, if we're talking about your current customers, we're talking about your current revenue stream. If you lose customers, you probably lose revenue, right?

Now, this presupposes that you're in a repeat customer business, and that's not true of everyone. There are certainly companies who sell just one thing on a one-time basis, without any likelihood of repeat business. Those companies still stand to benefit from the Third Level of Value – the value of *influence* – but I'll come back to that. The issue for right now is how to create and maintain happy customers, and the two keys to that challenge are *customer service* and *customer contact*.

Let's add two more adjectives to those two keys, *exceptional* customer service and *appropriate* customer contact.

Exceptional Service

How do you define exceptional customer service? I think your definition of exceptional customer service should relate to how you like to be treated when you're on the buying side of the equation – although I ran that idea past one of my clients recently, and she said: "I think I want our service to be one notch *above* what I'm willing to accept from my suppliers. I'm OK with 'adequate' customer service in most of what I buy."

I think that point is worth talking about some more. I found two definitions for *adequate* on dictionary.com:

1. As much or as good as necessary for some requirement or purpose; fully sufficient, suitable, or fit.
2. Barely sufficient or suitable.

In my experience, there's even a middle ground between these two definitions, and it's what most people seem to mean when they use the word in describing quality or service. According to #1, adequate means *exactly good enough*. According to #2, it means *barely good enough*. According to my middle ground, it means the quality or service was *fine*.

I'm reminded of an episode of The Big Bang Theory, in which Leonard says of *fine*: "Yeah, it's a perfectly good word. You put it in front of 'wine' or 'dining' and you've really got something." He wasn't talking about wine or dining, though, it was something much more personal (and intimate) between he and Penny. And *fine* meant *not really that good*, or more specifically, *not as good as I'd hoped it would be*.

That takes us to the best definition I've ever heard for exceptional customer service: *Quality or service which meets or exceeds the customer's expectations*.

Quality and Service

This brings up another important point. For the purposes of our discussion, *customer service* must include both the quality of the product and the quality of the service. As an example, in a restaurant, both the preparation of the food and the manner in which it is served contribute to the "happy customer" equation. Here's another example. You hire a yard care company to mow your lawn and trim your hedges. A crew comes out and does a less-than-adequate job. You complain to the owner, who comes out himself and re-does the work to your complete satisfaction. I'd call that *exceptional* customer service, even though the initial engagement was a pretty complete quality failure.

Here's still another important point. For the purposes of our discussion, *product* and *service* are not two different things. It's true that you can draw a distinction between companies which *manufacture* a product and companies which *provide* a service, but I want us to use the term *product* to encompass whatever it is that you sell. To put that another way, your *product* is *whatever it is that you get money in return for*. Whether it's tangible or intangible, physical or virtual, something that you call a product or something that you call a service, meeting or exceeding your customer's quality *and* service expectations is still critical to protecting the First Level of Value.

A quick aside. I wrote earlier about *mission* and *motto* (in regard to the Olympus Group's website). I'm just old enough to remember when General Electric used this motto: *Progress is our most important product!* You may be old enough to remember the motto they introduced in 1979 and used until about 2003: *We bring good things to life!*

GE's current mission statement: *General Electric Company's corporate mission is "to invent the next industrial era, to build, move, power and cure the world."* GE's current motto: *Imagination at work!*

That definitely reminds me of Brian's motto, which I still like better: *Imagine it. Done!*

Do You Have Happy Customers?

Now that we have a definition of *exceptional* customer service, let's get to the crux of the issue: *Are you providing it?* To put that another way: *Do you have happy customers?* To add to that: Do you have happy *and loyal* customers?

I asked a friend of a friend those questions at a social gathering a couple of years ago. His answer: "I assume so. I'm not hearing any complaints." I was reminded of that conversation recently when I learned that his company had gone out of business. My friend told me that the company had lost its biggest customer, and never recovered.

Now, I don't know all the details, but it certainly seems possible that this was not a happy customer, even back several years ago. And iti s definitely true that *"I'm not hearing any complaints"* is a really bad strategy for protecting the First Level of Value!

To paraphrase Yoda: *"Know or you do not know. There is no 'think' or 'hope' or 'assume'."*

It is critical that you have some sort of process for engaging with your customers to determine their level of satisfaction. Anything less than that and you're *risking*, not *protecting*.

Customer Contact

This is where *customer contact* comes in – *appropriate* customer contact – and it takes us back to something I wrote earlier. *It is never the buyer's responsibility to communicate with the seller. It is always the seller's responsibility to communicate with the buyer.*

As I wrote earlier, that actually means two things. One is that it's never their responsibility to *understand* what you're trying to communicate. It's your responsibility to make sure that the dots get connected, that real communication occurs. The other is that it's not your customers' responsibility to stay in touch with you. It's your responsibility to stay in touch with them!

Before I go any farther along this line, though, let's recognize that you can do just as much damage to a relationship with too much contact as too little. That's why *appropriate* is so important.

So how do we define *appropriate*? Here's my position. I think you should establish an *interval* for each customer, which is long enough to minimize the likelihood of smothering them, but short enough to minimize the possibility that something bad will happen – some sort of quality or service failure which would damage/threaten the relationship – and then never let that interval pass without either you hearing from them or them hearing from you.

I should specify two things. First, I'm mostly talking about *commercial* sales situations here, and as I hope you'll remember, that term refers mostly to situations where a salesperson is involved with a customer. Brian's company provides a good example. Every Olympus Group customer has a direct relationship with a salesperson, who is responsible, more than anything else, for the health and wellness of the relationship.

Every Customer?

The second thing is that I may not be talking about every customer – or, at least, the same sort of contact with every customer. This is a time management/prioritization issue. As I've noted, you already have plenty on your plate, and that probably means more tasks than you have hours in the day. With that in mind, some customers justify more direct contact. To put that differently, some customers simply have to be given less personal attention.

Do you have one of those 80/20 things going on, where 80% of your business comes from 20% of your customers? In that case, those critical customers probably require a shorter interval and more personal contact. That's probably true if you're 70/30, and there's something else to consider here. How about customers who are nowhere near maximized? One of my clients in Seattle does a little bit of business with Microsoft. I'm talking $5000 per year with a company which has several million dollars' worth of potential. I think you'll agree that the First Level of Value here is pretty important – because there ain't no Second Level or Third Level if there ain't no healthy First Level!

My best suggestion is to assign three categories of interval status. Category 1 is your critical customers and your best growth prospects. (Every current *customer* is a *prospect* to be a *maximized customer!*) Category 2 is made up of solid customers who you don't want to lose, but you simply have to take some risk because of your time management constraints. Category 3 is the catch-all for all the rest.

Category 1 customers get personal engagement for every interval contact – that means a phone call or even a personal visit. Category 2 customers get a mix of personal and less-personal – which would include email, text messaging and Social Media. Category 3 customers get "Customer Satisfaction Surveys," which I think of as *Better Than Nothing*.

Setting Your Intervals

Let's go back to the idea of setting an interval that is long enough to minimize the likelihood of smothering your customer, but short enough to minimize the possibility that something bad will happen – without you finding out about it while you still have the opportunity to *do something* about it!

Think back on my example of the yard care company owner who found out about a problem and then fixed it. He could have lost the customer, but he probably didn't. In fact, he probably created a happy *and* loyal customer. Here's a very fundamental idea: *When you screw up, you have a Golden Opportunity to reinforce your customer's original decision to buy from you.* Sure, you just showed them that you're not perfect, but now you have the chance to show them that you stand behind your product. Remember, this is all about *protecting* that First Level of Value.

Long enough and *short enough* are functions of how much they buy from you, and more specifically, how frequently they buy from you. Do you have a customer who places orders every week? If so, I don't think your interval should be any longer than two weeks. A week without orders could be an aberration, but it could also be a problem. Do you have a customer who places two orders a year, six months apart? If so, I think the interval should be six months – but within two weeks of when you'd expect those orders to be initiated.

(Please note my use of the word *initiated*. It's not uncommon for a conversation to start well before an order is actually placed. One of my clients runs two fundraising events every year, and they start talking with some of their suppliers a full year in advance. If a caterer, for example, called on them a month before the event, they'd be way too late to compete for that event.)

Here comes some good news. If you are setting these intervals correctly, you won't have to "invent" too many reasons to call these customers. For example, that customer who places orders every week? You're talking to them every week, just in the normal flow of the business you do with them. That provides regular opportunities for them to mention any issues or problems.

Don't leave that ball in their court, though. It has been proven in the marketplace that customers don't always tell you when they're unhappy. Sometimes they just "collect" small examples of unhappiness, until something – maybe just another little thing! – breaks the proverbial camel's back.

If I had a customer who generally placed orders every week, I would establish a two part program to protect the First Level of Value. First, the two week "have-we-heard-from-them?" interval. Second, a monthly check-in specifically to ask if there were any areas of dissatisfaction over the previous month, no matter how small.

This actually provides another engagement opportunity. I would say this to the customer: *"We have a lot going on every month. Thank you for your business by the way! I want to make sure than I don't let any problems fall through the cracks, so here's what I'd like to do. I'd like to call you on, say, the last business day of every month, just to ask if there's any way in which we've let you down over the last month. That way, I'll have the chance to correct it. How does that sound?"*

To put that another way: *"I'd like to help you to help me to protect our First Level of Value. Can we do that?"*

Follow Up Machine

This seems like a good time to remind you of something I wrote earlier: *Commercial selling is all about follow-up* – which has one of two purposes. In the context of *building* business, it's all about getting people to the next level. In the context we're talking about right now, it's all about *protecting* the relationship. Either way, it's critical that you have some means of managing your follow-up requirements. In other words, you need some sort of follow-up machine to remind you when it's time to make a sales call, a service call or an interval call.

Back to the *next level* for a moment. That might mean getting from an introductory email to a real conversation. It might mean getting from that conversation to being taken seriously. It might mean getting from being taken seriously to closing the first sale. It might mean getting from *customer* to *maximized customer*. Until you get to the *maximized customer* stage, there is always a next level! And even beyond that, there is risk attached to forgetting an interval call, and I want you to avoid that.

I use ACT! As my follow-up machine. ACT! was one of the first "contact management" software products, part of a category that's typically called CRM now – Customer Relationship Management. I go all the way back to the DOS version of the program, which I started using in 1991. Since then, ACT! has never once failed to remind me of something I told it I wanted to do.

Those last seven words are critical, though. Like any other computer application, *garbage in, garbage out* applies – *incorrect or poor quality input will always produce faulty output*. I'm sad to say that many of my clients have used their CRM's on a "part-time" basis. They were reminded of tasks they scheduled reminders for, but lots of other stuff fell through the cracks. I put *everything* in ACT!, or at least, everything I consider important. Maybe the best way to describe my relationship with my follow-up machine is that, if I do my job, it does its job, and I end up doing my job better.

Every day, ACT! provides me with a task list – everything I told it I wanted to do today. I don't always complete the list, but simply having the list makes it easier for me to make my daily – and sometimes hourly! – priority decisions. Sometimes that even means taking risk with a relationship, but when I do that, it's a conscious decision. Nothing falls through the cracks!

By the way, I would not be unhappy if you chose a different CRM. In fact, if I were starting from scratch today, I would probably choose OnePageCRM. I sometimes describe ACT! as a product that can do a hundred things, but I only need eight of them. OnePageCRM does about six of those things pretty well, and there are any number of similar products available. In my experience, the sheer complexity of "full-featured" CRM's like ACT! and salesforce.com deter some people from using them. There's a lot to be said for *simple* in this regard.

A quick note: I may have exaggerated when I told you that I put *everything* in ACT! Yesterday, I was reminded to make a First Level of Value call on someone I have on an eight-week interval. "Damn," I thought, "I saw that guy at the gym three weeks ago, and I failed to update ACT!" No big deal. I added appropriate notes on our conversation and bumped the reminder out five weeks to preserve the eight-week interval – and recommitted myself to doing my job with my CRM!

Call Content

Let's say you're reminded tomorrow to contact a Category 1 customer whom you have on an eight-week interval. What do you say on that call?

I'll answer that question by suggesting that you *not say* anything along the lines of: "Hey Dave, I haven't heard from you in a while." I get calls like that from my own suppliers, and I always feel like they're accusing me of cheating on them. "Hey Dave, I haven't heard from you for a while. Have you been messing around with my competitors?"

Granted, I may be overly sensitive to this particular possibility, but let's keep in mind that the goal here is to *protect* the First Level of Value, not to add any risk to the equation. Let's also keep in mind that "I haven't heard from you for a while" doesn't add any value to the relationship, even if it doesn't do any overt harm. I would tell any salesperson that it's OK to call me – or call on me – any time they have a good reason. I think, though, that you would join me in telling any salesperson not to bother us if they don't.

So what might represent *value* on an interval call? Do you have something new *and relevant* to tell me about? Do you have something "old" to remind me about? Back in my Moore Business Forms days, one of the values we provided was known as Forms Management – basically *inventory control*, to make sure our customers never ran out of the forms they needed. Sometimes that involved a physical inventory. I had customers I visited once each month to count all of the forms in their storerooms. We established minimum and maximum levels and tracked usage from month to month. When it was time to re-order a form – as a general rule, whenever we got close to just one month's supply remaining – I brought that information to the "owner" of that form, who made any changes that might be required and placed the order.

With some of my smaller customers, Forms Management took a different form. Instead of a monthly physical inventory, we set a "usage expectation" for every order. That was typically six months, because the rule of thumb at that time was that a six-month supply was the most cost-effective quantity to order. There were two factors involved in that calculation. The first was that, as with most manufactured products, the next one costs less to manufacture than the one before it. Ordering, say, 10,000 forms gave you a lower unit cost than ordering 5000 forms. The other factor was the possibility that the form would change. The "price break" on 10,000 forms could easily be lost if even a couple thousand of them had to be thrown away because they became obsolete.

Please note, though, that while six months' supply was typical, it was not absolute. In fact, the quantity discussion was a great opportunity for a customer engagement. "How many would you expect to use over six months?" I would ask. For the sake of discussion, let's make the answer 5000. Next question: "What is the likelihood that the form will change in six months?" Let's make the answer zero. Next question: "Can you see any likelihood that the form will change in a year, or even two years?" I had many situations where this sort of engagement resulted in a recommendation to buy a full years' supply, or even two years' supply of a form.

I didn't celebrate having generated a bigger order in those situations, by the way. I did celebrate doing the best thing for my customer. Truth be told, if a customer was going to use 20,000 forms over two years, it would be better for me to get that in four six-month orders. On one hand, I would make more money that way, and on the other hand, I'd have more frequent contact with my customer. Both of those things would represent value *to me*. But I always looked at this as another application of that Golden Rule.

Back to the Forms Management process with those smaller customers. We would set the "usage expectation," then I would schedule a call for halfway through that timeframe. If it was 5000 forms as a six-month supply, I'd set a follow-up call for three months, and the content of that call would be this: "When you placed the order, we expected that 5000 forms would last six months. Can I ask you to do a quick inventory. You should have 2500 forms left if we had the usage assumption correct."

From there, we'd modify the usage expectation – sometimes up and sometimes down – and I'd set a second follow-up call, halfway to when we expected to have to place the next order. Sometimes there would even be a third call required.

A reason to call. A *good* reason to call. A call that often filled an interval requirement. A call that *always* represented value.

Personal Content

This might also be an opportunity for a *personal* engagement that adds value to the relationship. It's widely accepted – and Brian has even noted in this book – that people like to buy from people they like, and the "like factor" is often connected to shared interest and common ground. I have always made it a point to identify and capture those shared/common opportunities – and in addition to being my follow-up machine, ACT! has been an ideal storage site for the data.

(That ties into another element of fundamental wisdom. I wrote earlier that the key to time management is to prioritize. The key to *organization* – which goes hand-in-hand with time management – is to put everything in its place. ACT! has been the "place" where I've stored all my relationship data over the years, for suspects, prospects, customers, maximized customers, suppliers, family and friends. I used to say that I couldn't run my business without ACT! The broader truth is that I couldn't run *my life* without my follow-up machine.)

(A related note: My brothers and I used to laugh at our father because (a) he was never without a pen and a notebook, and (b) he wrote down everything he thought he might want/need to remember. I do the same thing with my phone now, and all the data goes directly into ACT! I don't know if my daughter laughs at me … about that.)

Eclectic Interest

Here's some further advice about personal content. You should always be looking for the *most eclectic* interest you may share with another person. Here's an example. I have a client who has maybe 50 framed photos on his office walls, plus several other items which relate to either the New England Patriots or the Boston College Eagles. The photos include my client with several Patriots, my client in his BC uniform from his own playing days, and my clients' three sons in their high school football uniforms. There are also a series of smaller photos of his daughter playing various "kid roles" in the Boston Ballet's annual production of The Nutcracker.

It is no secret that this guy is a football guy. It is also no secret that he has interest in ballet, if only through his daughter's participation. But he told me once that I'm the only person who has ever engaged him, in his office, in a conversation about ballet. He also told me that's why he continued to engage with me, and took me seriously enough to eventually do business with me. (He didn't use the word *engage*, as I recall, but it's the right word, isn't it?)

Maybe I'm fortunate that I know something about ballet. It turns out that neither he nor I are really lovers of the artform, but my wife is a classically trained ballerina. She actually studied at Boston Ballet in their pre-professional program when she was in high school. So while others were "just another salesman who could talk to me about football," I was the one who stood out in the crowd.

Be on the lookout for an interest that will let you stand out in the crowd. And please consider this, you don't have to "share" the interest at the outset. You could probably learn enough about something to have a conversation about it. You could even engage your suspect/prospect/customer to be your teacher. I had another client once who had a copy of Sport Parachutist magazine on the corner of his desk. I asked him if he was a skydiver. Then I told him I'd always wanted to try it, and asked him how he got started?

For what it's worth, I never did try it, and he teased me for years about my lack of courage. I still believe, though, that an at-least-temporary shared interest in parachuting helped me get that relationship off the ground.

Thank You!

Even if you can't come up with something eclectic, a shared interest can still be the basis for an interval call. For example, I wouldn't have hesitated to talk about football if I needed a reason to call, and there was simply no ballet-related reason available. But think about this, depending on the timing, I might have found my way to a newspaper story about his sons' high school football team. With any luck, the story would mention one of the sons, and I could call and say: "Hey, I understand (your son, by name) made a big play Friday night. You must be pretty proud!" (Rule of Thumb: Most people like talking about their kids, especially when their kids have done something to be proud of!) What if I needed to make an interval call and it wasn't football season? I could still look up whatever sport was in season, just in case one of the sons played that sport too and did something noteworthy. I could even look into what was going on with BC football in the offseason.

As noted, if you set the intervals correctly, you probably won't have to invent too many reasons to make your interval calls. The normal flow of business will take care of it for you.

One more thought on this topic. If you can't come up with any better reason, you can say something like this: *"Hey, I was thinking about you this morning, and it occurred to me that it may have been too long since I called you and thanked you for your business. You are very important to me/us, and I/we appreciate the trust you place in us. Just wanted to tell you that."*

Second Level

What's important about the First Level of Value is that you protect it. What's important about the Second Level of Value is that you *proact* it. I may have just invented that word, but I can't think of any reason there shouldn't be a verb form of *proactive*.

Again, *customer contact* has a role to play in this element of Customer Maximization, but perhaps the larger issue is *customer education*. Here's a question: *How good a job do you think your best customer would do of defining your product line?* By that, I mean listing every single product or service that he or she could be/should be buying from you. That's an easy question to answer if you only sell one or two things, but it gets much more complex the more things you sell.

Even the fitness club example from much earlier provides an example of what I'm talking about. I'd bet that most of the club's members know that personal trainers are available for, well, personal – read that: individual, one-on-one – training. I'd bet that less than half, though, know that you can put your own small group together and engage a personal trainer to work with you as a group. I'd even bet that less than half know that there's a page on the club's website where you can buy gear with the club's logo. (I've never figured out why they don't have that same gear for sale inside the club!)

I used to work for a guy who believed that *"I didn't know you could do that"* was the worst thing a salesperson could hear from a customer. He was talking about lost opportunity; the customer buying from someone else because they didn't know they could buy it from you. I saw the wisdom in what he was saying, but later decided that those words are the *best thing* a salesperson can hear from a customer – *provided that* the salesperson initiates the conversation that makes the customer say the words. *Customer education* plants the seeds of future opportunity.

This is an area where many commercial salespeople make a classic mistake. One of my clients sells cleaning supplies, and for years, their salespeople were taught to ask customers: *"What other cleaning supplies do you buy?"* That's a terrible question, because it leaves it up to the customer to define what encompasses cleaning supplies. Did you know, for example, that most commercial cleaning supplies companies sell clothing? They sell shoes and gloves and heavyweight pants and shirts – the kind of things cleaners/janitors wear. Many can even sell you heavyweight shirts with your company's logo and your cleaners' names embroidered on the chest. A question about "cleaning supplies" probably wouldn't cover that, would it?

About three years ago, we developed a new process to address *Customer Maximization*. First, we assigned each customer an appropriate contact interval. Second, we made a list of the various subcategories of cleaning supplies and other elements of their product line. It included:

- Floor cleaning
- Wall cleaning
- Window cleaning
- Air cleaning
- Kitchen cleaning
- Food handling
- Bathroom cleaning
- Chemical handling
- Paper goods
- Storage goods
- Apparel
- Miscellaneous

The third step was to create a spreadsheet to be used as a "visibility and input" document. Column A was the name of the company. Column B was the name of the customer – the individual who placed orders with my client. Column C was the title of the customer. Column D was the contact interval. Then, Columns E-P were headed by the various subcategories.

The fourth step was to evaluate each customer, line by line, to determine which subcategories they were already buying, and to identify, by process of elimination, which subcategories we should make sure to educate them about.

Over the next few months, the salespeople engaged in many conversations which followed along these lines: *"Dave, I've done some research into what you've been buying from us. You've bought a lot of Product A, and a little bit of Product B, but you've never bought any of Product C. I wanted to ask you, do you have any need or application for Product C in your cleaning and maintenance operations?"*

As the salespeople learned, there are really only three possible answers to that sort of question:

1. *"Oh, God, no! We've never used Product C. We don't want to use Product C. We'd rather die than have any involvement with Product C!"* No, it never happened quite like that, but the point is, sometimes there just isn't any opportunity with a particular product. But, would you agree (with Yoda) that it's better to know than to not know?

2. *"I buy a lot of Product C, and I didn't know I could buy it from you. And that's great news, because I like you, and I hate the people I buy Product C from now."* No, it never happened quite like that either, but it is simply true that sometimes all you have to do is to educate your customer. (Wait, what's that you say? You've mentioned Product C to your customer on more than one occasion? They *should* know that they could be buying it from you? I won't argue that point, except to say that you obviously didn't fully engage or communicate. Your fault or their fault, it doesn't really matter – except please remember what I've said about it never being their responsibility to *communicate* with you. And please also consider this. Is it possible that you mentioned Product C along with Products D, E, F, G and so on? Here's another fundamental idea: *The more you try to jam into any single engagement, the less likely it is that your counterpart will hear and register all of it, or even most of it.*

3. "I don't use any Product C, but I can tell you who does."

That last one is my segue into the Third Level of Value, but let me say this before we go there. *Customer education* is a legitimate reason for an interval call, but that's probably not as proactive as I want you to be. If I identified three or four product opportunities with one of my customers, I would first ask myself, which one would seem the be the greatest opportunity? Then I'd rank the rest of them in order of importance. Then I'd tell my follow-up machine when I want to talk with the customer about each of the product opportunities, spreading them out to avoid trying to do too much in any single engagement. Then, when reminded by my follow-up machine, I'd make those calls, in the expectation that I'll find a few dry holes and a few real opportunities to *proact* the Second Level of Value.

Third Level

The Third Level of Value is the value of *influence*; the way(s) in which current customers can help you to develop new customers. What's important about the Third Level of Value is that you *fully leverage* it. There are two main categories of *influence*: referrals and testimonials.

I find it interesting that the term "testimonial" has become outdated. The more common terminology these days seems to be "customer review." That's what they're called on amazon.com and other websites.

Ultimately, the terminology doesn't matter. No matter what you call it, there is tremendous power in having a buyer say something good about a product or a seller.

So, if you're the seller, your Customer Maximization plan should include a *proactive* effort to generate *positive* customer reviews. Just remember, they don't do you any good if they're invisible.

This is another area in which the Olympus Group website does a good job. First of all, there's a "Customer Testimonials" page. (OG is Old School, using the old terminology!) In addition to a few glowing testimonials, it says this on that page:

We are privileged to work with some great companies

We work with some amazing companies on their exciting projects, and we love to see them in action! If you've had a great experience with Olympus, share it with us! By sharing your story, we'll thank you with:

- *A link to your brand's page on our website, which averages 3,400 page views per month*
- *A possible feature in our monthly eNewsletter circulated to 10,000+ recipients*

We take pride in our creations. We hope you do too!

Key point: Olympus Group offers an *incentive* for happy customers to tell their Third Level of Value stories. Prominently placed on the page, there are tabs which lead to testimonials about Custom Printing, and about Mascots, and a tab which invites – and provides a template for – customers to write their own testimonials.

Another key point: Brian doesn't leave it up to happy customers to find this page. It is well understood that it's part of each salesperson's job to (1) ensure that customer expectations were met or exceeded, and (2) invite happy customers to participate in the testimonial process. It's never high pressure! Again, the foundation of Customer Maximization is to *protect* the First Level of Value. But since testimonials have value, and you want to maximize value, you should always – when it is appropriate! – ask.

Referrals

I've gotten into the habit of asking this question whenever I speak to an audience of salespeople or small business owners: "How many of you have gained a new customer recently through a referral?" Typically, more than half of the audience will raise their hands.

Then I ask a second question: "Was it an *active* or *passive* referral?"

Here's the difference. *Passive* describes the kind of referral in which someone says something nice about you, probably without you even knowing about it, and that leads someone else to start an engagement with you and ultimately buy from you. *Active* describes the process by which you ask your customers if they know *anyone else* who might be interested in buying from you.

Let me make this clear. Both types of referrals are good. Very good! But if all you're getting are *passive* referrals, you're missing out on a very key element of the Third Level of Value.

So let's make it a rule that you should always make sure that you have happy customers, and you should always at least consider asking every happy customer if they know someone who might benefit from doing business with you in the same way that they do. Please note, by the way, that I'm not saying that you should actually pursue referrals from every happy customer. I can remember several times in my own career when it just felt like a bad move for one reason or another. I guess what I am saying is that I think your default position should be "go for it" – unless there seems to be a good reason not to.

This is another area where many salespeople make a classic mistake, though, especially with what I like to call *internal* referrals. They'll go to their customer and ask: *"Who else here buys (what I sell)?"* That's a terrible question, because again, it leaves it up to the customer to define the product line.

But it's also a terrible question because, the bigger the organization, the less likely it is that any left hand will know what the right hand is doing.

Tracking Titles

This is where the importance of titles re-enters our discussion. Think back to the spreadsheet I developed with my cleaning supplies client. Do you remember that Column C was for the title of the customer? One of the things that became visible when this spreadsheet was completed was that nearly 90% of their customer base had one of seven titles:

- Purchasing Manager
- Facility Manager
- Maintenance Manager
- Housekeeping Manager
- Kitchen Manager
- Human Resources Manager
- Chief Cook & Bottle Washer

In some cases, these were formal titles. In other cases, they were "hats" – and you know all about wearing multiple hats, right? In the smallest businesses, one person might wear all of these hats. That's where the expression Chief Cook and Bottle Washer comes from. (I went looking online for the etymology of the phrase. The best I could find was a reference to the 1830's and "someone whose responsibilities include absolutely everything, from the highest level to the lowest." All I do know for sure is that it was one of my father's favorite expressions to describe his role as a partner in a small business.)

Anyway, *"who else here buys (what I sell)?"* is the wrong question. A much better strategy is to identify which titles or hats you are already selling to, and then ask specially for a referral to the person/people who carry the other titles or wear the other hats. In other words, if you're selling to the Facility Manager but not the Human Resources Manager, the question is: *"Who's in charge of Human Resources?"*

One more thing. Referrals are great, whether reactive or proactive, but there's something that's even better. That would be an *introduction*. If you find out who's in charge of Human Resources, you're positioned to make what most salespeople would refer to as a *warm call*. And that's definitely warmer than a cold call, but let's not pretend that it's always the ideal temperature. To my way of thinking, a cold call might be 32 degrees, a referral-led warm call might be 50 degrees, but an introduction might well get you to 72 degrees. Which temperature would you prefer?

I have often asked customers if they'd be willing to walk me over and introduce me to another title or hat. That wasn't always reasonable or even possible, but that just meant on to Plan B: *"Would you be willing to make a call or fire off an email to let him/her know that I'll be calling?"* My philosophy has always been that *warm is always better* in selling.

Measuring Temperature

Speaking of temperature, I built a Customer Maximization spreadsheet with another client recently, and we added another column to measure the current state of the relationship. This became Column D, in between the title of the customer and the interval we'd established. The data point we entered was based on the idea that 98.6 degrees would represent a *happy and loyal* customer – a solid relationship, not at risk in any way at the current time. Anything higher than that – for example, 104 degrees – would represent a solid relationship that went beyond meeting or exceeding their expectations. As my client put it: "They like us enough to give us another chance, even if we screw up big time."

Anything less than 98.6 would indicate a relationship at risk. 90 degrees might mean that the last order didn't go smoothly, or maybe that some risk had to be taken in terms of prioritizing that customer against all of the other things that were on the seller's plate on a particular day. 80 degrees might mean that the last order went *badly*, or that something really important fell through the cracks.

I used the term "visibility and input" earlier to describe this sort of spreadsheet. Remember, I want you to have a follow-up machine. I *don't* want you to rely on a spreadsheet to perform that function. But, it has been my experience that "in writing" is the best way to arrange all the data before you enter it into your follow-up machine. Visibility *then* input.

Advertising To Customers

I wrote earlier – all the way back in Chapter One! – that a one-size-fits-all advertising strategy is unlikely to work for you. There are four categories of people on the buying side of your sales equation – suspects, prospects, customers and maximized customers – and you should engage each of them differently.

The "suspect message" should be all about separating your likely suspects from the people who will never, ever buy from you. *"Are you at all interested in (what we sell)?"* If there is interest, the next stage of the process is to motivate movement toward The Point Of Sale.

The "prospect message" should be all about getting fully qualified prospects to place that first order. I see this more as a "selling" challenge than an "advertising" challenge – in other words, there will often be a salesperson involved. Still, there are ways that "advertising" can support the sales effort. For example, one of my clients has both a *suspect* version and a *prospect* version of a direct mailer. If the *suspect* mailer generates interest, but the salesperson's involvement doesn't result in an immediate sale, the *prospect* mailer goes out – providing more than just *"are you at all interested"* detail. She also has a version of the *prospect* mailer which contains a coupon, to provide an incentive to pull the trigger on the first order.

The "customer message" should have two – or perhaps three – elements: (1) Thank you for your business, (2) please buy from us again, and if appropriate, (3) please consider some of our other products or services. Hmmm, would a coupon be appropriate to provide some incentive towards #3?

Actually, I should probably ask whether you think a coupon would be appropriate to provide some incentive toward #2 as well? Here's what I think. If the product they bought met or exceeded their expectations, you shouldn't have to provide any further incentive to buy it again. If they like your pizza, you shouldn't have to make the next pizza they buy from you *less profitable*, should you?

Having said that, I suppose you could consider the "re-order coupon" a reward, or you could consider it a tool to help you "lock up" the next order. Both of those things provide some value to both seller and buyer. But let's not lose sight of The Prime Directive: To run a profitable business. Don't give your profit away without a good reason.

Now to the "maximized customer message." If they are truly maximized customers – in other words, if you're really getting *all of the value* from the relationship – the only required message is *Thank You!*

12 Value vs. Pain
Dave Fellman

Value has been a recurring theme in this book. Brian and I have written about bringing it, maximizing it and recognizing it. We have also stressed that value is always defined by the party that receives it, not the party that provides it. Yes, as the seller – or the employer – you are supposed to spend time thinking about how you bring/provide value, and you are allowed to talk about that perception of value during the selling process. But the ultimate decision still rests with the buyer.

Let's consider the "selling" that goes on between employer and employee. As the employer, you are selling the idea that "this is a good job." And I'm not just talking about selling this idea to prospective new employees. The truth is, you have to sell it to your current employees every day. And this kind of "commerce" only works if they're buying what you're selling, right?

Employer: "This is a good job. I pay you well, provide excellent working conditions, and meaningful benefits."

Employee: "I'm not buying it. I don't feel that way at all."

Does that sound like a healthy relationship with an engaged employee? Hopefully, it reinforces everything that Brian has written about giving your employees a voice. Because when they have a voice, you can have a *dialogue*, and these *disengagement* issues can be identified, discussed and hopefully resolved.

Here's another way to look at this. Your perspective rules in matters of performance. You ultimately get to decide whether an employee is *doing* a good job. But they get to decide if you're *providing* one.

Customers and Prospects

As the "sales guy" in this writing team, I tend to be focused mostly on *value* as it applies to customers and prospects. I've had some interesting conversations with buyers over the years about their perception of value. I've also learned that they tend to think of *value* in close relationship to *pain*.

The juxtaposition of those two influences seemed to be worth consideration, so back a few years ago, I started building a list of people who buy things and calling them to ask about their perceptions of value and pain.

(Obviously, pretty much everybody buys things. My study was mostly oriented toward B2B buying, but a few of the people I talked to brought their personal purchasing into the discussion. I'm pretty confident that we can apply the findings to both B2B and B2C.)

Here are my findings, expresses as a dual listing of the Top 10 Things Buyers Perceive As Value, and the Top 10 Things (They) Perceive As Pain. I'm also including "explanatory" quotes from some of the buyers I interviewed for this study.

The Value List

1. **Advice:** "I'm an expert in the stuff I sell, but I'm hardly an expert in most of the stuff I buy. I want the people I buy from to be able to give me the same sort of knowledge-based advice I give my own customers. Don't just sell me stuff, help me buy the right stuff!"

2. **Familiarity:** "The more any supplier knows about our business and the way we do business, the better they'll understand and be able to meet our needs."

3. **Absolute Honesty:** "Don't hide bad news from me, and don't ever put me in a situation where it's the last minute and I don't have any options. If you can't do something, tell me up front, or else the very minute after you realize we've got a problem."

4. **Price:** "You don't have to have the lowest price, although you do have to be competitive. The more you give me in terms of overall value, the more I'm willing to pay."

5. **Dependable Quality:** "I want all of my orders to look just as good as those samples you've shown me."

6. **Sensitivity:** "You have to understand that I don't set the deadlines, they're imposed on me by the people I work for. I understand that I cause problems for you, but you need to understand that I'm really passing along a problem that's been dropped on me. If you can help me solve my problem, I'll love you."

7. Additional Services: "When I find someone I like doing business with, I want to do as much business with them as I can. You can't believe how excited I was when I learned that my website guy could also help me to design our catalogs."

8. Desire: "You can see the difference in service when a company really wants you as a customer. I've worked with some who never showed me that, and that's why I don't work with them anymore."

9. Flexibility: "The only constant in my business is how fast things change. I need suppliers who can keep up with the change."

10. Predictability: "I want to know what I'm getting, in terms of quality, service, everything. If I can count on that, I'm a very happy camper."

The Pain List
1. Complicating My Life. "I have a million things going on a good day, and the fact of the matter is that I need help. I need suppliers who will simplify my life, not make it more complicated. I'm even willing to pay more for a helpful supplier, but I won't keep on using one who makes things worse instead of better."

2. Unreliable/Inconsistent Service: "I need to know that I can trust you to deliver on time, and to keep me advised about any problems so they don't turn into bigger problems."

3. Unreliable/Inconsistent Quality: "Nothing makes me crazier than when one job looks great and then the next one looks awful. It is really that hard to produce consistent quality?"

4. Miscommunication/Untimely Communication: "It's hard to trust a salesperson who tells you one thing and then a completely different thing happens. And why do they always wait until the very last minute to tell you about a problem?"

5. Problems With Digital Files: "I still don't understand why a file that looks fine to us won't work for them. Aren't they supposed to be the experts? If we're doing it wrong, teach us how to do it right!"

6. Untrained Salespeople: "I think I know more about the product than my salesperson does, and I probably know more about selling too. She's nice enough, I guess, but she's really not good for much more than picking up orders and having someone from her office call me back to answer my questions."

7. Additional Charges: "I award the job based on the quoted price, and then I find out that it's a whole different price. If you want to keep my business, you'd better be able to tell me up front how much it's going to cost, and spell out all the possibilities for additional charges so I can avoid them."

8. Procedures Violations: "We have proscribed ways of doing things— requisitions, purchase orders, shipping standards and a requirement for a packing list with every delivery. All our suppliers know this, but they still mess up our procedures most of the time."

9. Lack Of Responsiveness: "There generally are only two times when I'll call a salesperson —when I have something (an order) for them or when I need something from them. Either way, I want to hear back from them quickly."

10. Lack of Empathy: "If my suppliers had to walk in my shoes for a while, I think they'd understand why I'm a 'demanding' customer. I try to understand their problems, but they have to understand mine too."

Two Sides Of The Coin

I think the thing that struck me most about these conversations with buyers is that their perceptions of value and pain reflect two sides of the same coin. In other words, if you give them what they're looking for they look at that as value, and if you don't give them what they're looking for, they experience it as pain. So, as Yogi Berra might have said, "All you have to do to have happy customers is to make them happy."

13 Engaging With Suppliers
Dave Fellman

I wrote earlier that your business is all about selling something to somebody. Once that happens, your business becomes all about producing and delivering whatever it is that you sell. During the selling stage, the critical engagement is between the seller (you) and the buyer. During the production/delivery stage, the critical engagement is between the seller (you) and the producers – in other words, your team.

It's time now to talk about a third stage, which we might call the "stuff" stage. This stage encompasses all of the "stuff" that surrounds the other two, including everything from the raw materials that go into your product to the supplies that your team members use as they do their jobs. The critical engagement in this stage is between the seller (you) and the *other* seller.

You are still the seller, because your business is all about selling something to somebody, right? But in this stage, you are also the buyer, dealing with the all of those *other* sellers! The key to real success at this stage may be to apply the same standards to yourself as a customer that you do to your own actual customers. In other words, follow the Golden Rule about treating others the way you would like them to treat you.

Good Customers

How do you define a good customer? I would imagine that sales volume is at, or at least close, to the top of the list. But please consider that *big* customers are not always *best* customers. For example, one of my clients does business in both the public and private sectors. Her Number 1, 2 and 4 customers in terms of sales volume are government entities. It's all bid work, and while the dollars are substantial, the profit margins are not. Her Number 8, 9 and 10 customers in terms of sales volume actually contribute more profit dollars to her business than 1, 2 and 4.

The government agencies are still *good* customers, but she's very aware of the difference between *good* and *great*. Her goal, in fact, is to move 2 and 4 into the 5-10 range – not by doing less business with them, but by adding new high volume/high profit customers, and/or growing some of her smaller-but-more-profitable customers into the 2-4 range. For what it's worth, her Number 1 customer is so much larger in terms of sales volume that it's unlikely they will be overtaken. And while the margins are not spectacular, the volume and even limited gross profit does cover a lot of overhead.

A quick – but important! – follow-up on that statement. A high volume/low profit customer can be *part of* a solid foundation for a business. But too many businesses have failed because they *only had* low profit customers. The argument that high volume/low profit can cover a lot of overhead is only valid once a company reaches its break-even point. Up until that point, low profit only contributes to loss.

Third Factor

I think *contribution to profit* should be the most important factor in defining a good customer, with sales volume probably second. The third factor ties into my definition of a *bad* customer, which goes like this: *Anyone who is more trouble than they're worth is a bad customer!* (I think Brian would agree, by the way, that any employee who is more trouble than they're worth is a bad employee!) The critical question regarding bad customers and bad employees is pretty straightforward: *What are you going to do about it?* Before I go there, though, a reminder that the point of this chapter is *don't be a bad customer!*

Why is that important? As I wrote earlier, at the most fundamental level, all business is transactional. At the highest level, though, we want it to be relational. That means customers who *want to* buy from us, employees who *want to* work for us, and suppliers who really want to work *with* us. *With* is the key word regarding suppliers. In my experience, *selling to you* and *working with you* tend to be two very different things, and that's especially important when you think you need a drill bit and your supplier realizes that what you really need is a hole!

Are you an expert on (fill in the blank)? If so, you can probably make an informed buying decision without much help from a supplier of that product or service. If you're not an expert, it's a whole different story, right?

Sometimes expertise is not the issue. Maybe it's the most basic of commodity products, but you need an above-and-beyond level of service from your supplier in order to meet or exceed your own customer's wants or needs. Maybe it's one of those situations where *you* are Customer B and your supplier also has a Customer A who wants/needs the same level of service, but there's not enough time – or maybe even enough of the product available – to make both of you happy.

Who gets what they need? In most cases, the good customer. Who ends up with a problem? In most cases, the bad one. Please note, by the way, that *bad* is a relative term here. If you're not the *best* customer, you're at risk if push ever comes to shove.

Bad Customers

OK, let's step away from engaging with your suppliers for just a moment. Let's say that *you* have a bad customer. They are more trouble than they're worth. What are you going to do about it?

First, I strongly recommend that you sit yourself down in a quiet place and invest a few minutes in thinking through *exactly* why they're more trouble than they're worth. This is not a situation where a vague sense of dissatisfaction is enough to act on. Because something has to be done, and that something involves a binary choice. You can fire the customer. Or, you can change the more-trouble-than-they're-worth equation.

Wait, I suppose there is a third choice. You can do nothing. You can *tolerate* bad behavior. But is that doing your business any good? Unfortunately, it seems that this is what happens in most bad customer situations. It doesn't have to be, though. A bad customer situation is an *engagement* opportunity.

So, back to the binary options. You may have to fire the customer, but I want that to be Plan B. First, I would like you to see if you can change their behavior. Make a list of the specific issues. Give some thought to what would be satisfactory improvement. Then see if you can set up an opportunity to talk about the problem(s).

I have been involved in a lot of these conversations over the years. I always start them the same way: *Thank you for your business!* I always continue and say: *"I'd like/we'd like to continue to do business with you, maybe even* more *business. But I/we have noticed that things don't always go smoothly when we do business together, and you've probably noticed the same thing. Can we talk about those rough edges and maybe smooth them out a little?"*

From there, you will hopefully find resolution. It may not be perfect, but it may be enough to tilt the relationship toward an acceptable balance. *Better*, in most cases, is a satisfactory outcome.

If not, you may have to fire the customer. In my experience, it's not always possible to change their behavior, but it's always worth trying. And if it does come to firing, take some comfort in this idea: *Let's let the bad customers weaken our competitors!*

Think about that. The more time and other resources your competitors have to spend taking care of bad customers, the less time and other resources they have available to compete for your good customers. Beyond that, the more time and other resources they have to spend on bad customers, the more likely it is that they'll *fail to meet or exceed* the expectations of their own best customers, maybe putting those customers in play for you. There's no upside to tolerating bad customer behavior, and all too much downside.

Back To Suppliers

There's no upside to tolerating bad customer behavior, and all too much downside. To put that in *seller* and *other seller* context, there's no upside and plenty of downside for you in being a bad customer. *You do not want to be more trouble than you're worth to any of your suppliers, especially your most important suppliers!*

To extend that, there's also no upside for you in dealing with bad suppliers. So how about if we say this, whether you're buyer or seller – *seller* or *other seller* – you should take full responsibility for all of the relationships that are important to your business. If that means you lead the way in developing true partnerships with your suppliers, so be it. Look at this as *another* engagement opportunity.

Here's how you might structure the conversation:

- Let me tell you what I like most about doing business with you.
- Let me tell you what I like least about doing business with you.
- Now you tell me the same things, what you like most and least about me/us.
- Now you tell me what else you think we should be talking about, so that both of us get maximum value from our relationship.

Everything Changes

This seems like a good time to come back to something I wrote earlier, and promised to expand upon. *Everything changes*, I wrote. *That would seem to leave you with two choices. You can change with the times, or you can defend your position. Thankfully, there's a third choice. You can do both!*

The context I was writing about was dealing with Millennials, but I think the statement refers to all of the things we do to communicate with suspects, prospects, customers, maximized customers, employees and suppliers – of any generation. To me, it always comes down to a single question: *What's the best way to do this?*

Here's an example. Your customer – let's make her a Millennial – prefers e-mail to any other form of communication. You have something complex to discuss with her, so you call her on the phone. You end up leaving a voice mail message, and she responds via e-mail, saying: "Just tell me what you need via email." On one hand, writing a comprehensive email might take you a significant amount of time, and a comprehensive reply might take her a significant amount of time, but five minutes on the telephone might wrap the whole thing up. So do you (a) write the email, or (b) respond to this email saying something like "I understand that email is your preferred method of communication, but I really believe that we can both handle this issue more efficiently with a five minute phone call. Can I convince you to do it my way this time?"

Here's another example. Your supplier – let's make him a Baby Boomer – prefers to talk on the phone, and every conversation runs longer than it needs to because he tends to want to socialize, and he also tends to be disorganized. Should you (a) allow this *status quo* to continue, or (b) insist on communicating more efficiently via email or text?

My answer to both examples is *I don't know*. In some cases, the best choice is to push to do it your way. In others, it's to concede to do it their way. In still others, it's to meet in the middle – or to find a different method altogether.

The point is that you sometimes have to engage on how best to engage. There's no one-size-fits-all in terms of communication strategy. But any time there's conflict, there's an opportunity to get closer together or farther away. Any question about what's usually better?

****

Now, this started out as my chapter, but Brian has some perspective on engaging with suppliers too. Not to mention a whole lot more direct experience at this than I have! Brian, take it away…

****

Brian On Engaging with Suppliers

Thanks, Dave. OK, it's pretty easy to understand the need for engaging with customers and engaging with your employees. Customers help drive business and employees help get the product out the door. It's important, though, not to ignore the value of engaged suppliers. Before I get to that, a little review and amplification. Starting with a question: *What exactly is an engaged customer?* Let's define that as someone who views the relationship with you, your product, or your brand as more than merely transactional. They perceive additional value, above and beyond the transactional baseline of "I give you money and you give me a product."

How does one get to be an engaged customer? It happens for a variety of reasons – a great sales experience, a knowledgeable salesperson or a brand they can identify with and believe in. Dave wrote earlier about *maximized* customers. That's related to, but not exactly the same as my definition of *engaged*. Here's the difference. *Engaged* customers very often become advocates, they help drive new sales in addition to keeping you in business with their own purchases. *Engaged* customers can be your best sales assets, referring and recommending you to their own contacts. And I'm really talking here about when they do it on their own, with no effort on your part. Dave made the point that you can and should work proactively at gaining referrals and recommendations, but I bet you'll agree that it's even better when you don't have to work so hard!

I have mostly focused on engaging with employees throughout this book. I hope I've convinced you that engaged employees care more, work harder and do better work. But it all ties together. If you have engaged employees, you are much more likely to have engaged customers. Let me ask you – again! – to think about Southwest Airlines. Obviously, I have a great deal of respect for them. Their employees seem very engaged, they seem to enjoy their jobs and appreciate the company they work for. This is evident in how they approach their roles, from whimsical safety briefings to going above and beyond to recognize the birthdays of their passengers. Engaged employees leads to engaged customers, and that has led Southwest to the strongest financial performance of any major domestic airline over the past 20 years.

Engaged Suppliers

Now let's talk about engaging with suppliers. And let's be clear, I'm not talking about simply fielding a sales call from a vendor or supplier. This is about *truly engaging* with the people and companies you buy from.

I've interviewed numerous salespeople over the years who referred to themselves as relationship-based sellers. *"I add value by building relationships with key customers and becoming a resource for them."* But I can't think of one time where a candidate interviewing for a purchasing role said anything like this: *"I build relationships with key suppliers and leverage these relationship to benefit the company."*

As sellers, we often complain that buyers view us as commodities – and that "us" includes our companies, our products, and even us as individuals. That mindset very often leads them to make buying decisions based solely on price. Think about the way purchasing departments typically operate. The "buyers" are tasked with cutting the company's annual spend, year over year. A purchasing department's primary goal is usually to cut costs, and the easiest way to do this is to push suppliers to cut prices.

I know that we have been guilty of this at Olympus, but what if we tasked our purchasing team to *engage* with the suppliers, the same way we ask our sales team to engage with customers? I frequently ask the sales team specific questions on how their levels of engagement are going with key customers. I often join sales team members on key sales calls. What if I start asking my purchasing team members questions like this – *"Hey, did you have any meaningful conversations reflecting high levels of engagement with any of our suppliers today?"* What if I start sitting in on some of their "sales" meetings as well?

Old model: A purchasing agent is tasked with cutting costs, and brings in several possible suppliers, entertains their sales pitch, and invites them to offer a quote. (Or maybe to participate in the dreaded reverse auction!) In all of these scenarios, there is one primary objective – to drive out cost and find the lowest price/bidder. This has proven to be a very effective method in identifying the supplier with the lowest price.

New model: A purchasing agent is tasked with getting to know both current and potential new suppliers personally, and understanding the full breadth of their products and services. We don't just invite a quote; instead, we describe our issues and challenges and invite a proposal: *"What do you suggest we do that would give us a better result?"* One likely result of this strategy is that our suppliers are now adding value beyond price, and we are now making more intelligent sourcing decisions.

McKinsey & Company, one of the most successful management consulting firms, and a thought leader in business strategy, published an article in 2019 titled: "The New Roles of Leaders in the 21st Century." The article explains how, in traditional organizations, the leaders primary focus is to maximize shareholder value. The new role of leaders, according to McKinsey is to focus on *co-creating* value, with and for ALL stakeholders, expanding beyond shareholders to include customers, employees, partners and suppliers. In today's market, for long-term sustained success, everyone must win – including suppliers!

Case Study

I had my own eyes opened wide about seven years ago. I was on a routine sales call in Atlanta, visiting with the Creative Director of one of our largest customers. He and I had a great relationship. We would play tennis and grab a beer outside of work, knew one another's families, and had worked well together for years. As a customer, they were absolutely critical to our business. But on this particular day, I could tell something was off – he was not himself, and then he dropped a bombshell on me.

"Hey Brian, you know how you ship all of our POP (point of purchase graphics) to a centralized distribution center?"

"Yes." (It's pretty common with our retail customers to ship all of the POP graphics to a distribution center, which then handles allocation to the individual stores.)

"Well, we just signed an agreement with a new company and there's a small change. Not only do they manage the distribution of the POP, but they also manage the procurement of the graphics."

Now I'm a little shocked. *"They do what?!?!?"*

"They are now responsible for buying everything you currently sell to us. It all goes through them now."

And just like that, it looked like we might be losing one of our largest customers overnight!

More To The Story

Fortunately, the story didn't end there. My friend/customer introduced me to James, one the executives at this new organization. James was great, certainly different than most buyers – and very different from what I expected. He spent hours with us and took the time to learn about our business and our capabilities. In other words, James took the time to *engage* with a supplier.

We started working with James, and our business actually grew a little. But after 6-months, he called to schedule a year-end review meeting, at our facility. I feared the worst, expecting that the purpose of his visit was to secure pricing concessions, perhaps volume discounts. To my surprise, James simply asked: "How's the business going for you? Is it working, is it profitable?"

I didn't know quite how to answer. It was profitable, and the relationship was great, but before responding, I felt like I needed to vet the question. "Why do you ask, James? I don't think I've ever been asked that by a customer before."

His answer was sincere, and clearly demonstrated his attitude of engagement with his suppliers. "Brian, if the business is not working for you and you're not profitable, that means this model is not working, and we'd need to put our heads together to make some changes. For my company to be successful, we need this business model to work for everyone, including our key suppliers, and last I checked Olympus was a 'for-profit' business. I simply want to make sure it's working out."

I had to laugh. Here I feared the worst, and he just wanted to make sure we were as happy with the relationship as he was, that we were making money so we'd be around to work with him in the future. I learned a great lesson that day, and it caused me to reflect back on previous mistakes I'd made in not engaging as well with our own suppliers.

James has remained a friend, and remains engaged with us, and has been one of our largest and most important accounts to this day.

Another Example

A friend of mine named Robbie runs a large format printing company in the Atlanta area. It's very similar to Olympus, so Robbie faces most of the same challenges we face, and, in fact, that most printers face:

- Downward pricing pressure
- Decreased lead-times
- Material price increases
- Large inventories eating up capital and precious manufacturing space

On a visit to his facility, I noted that it looked very different. Gone were the usual racks and racks of material. His plant looked almost empty. I actually feared that he'd lost a key customer, or experienced some other serious downturn in business. When I asked him how things were going, his answer shocked me.

"We're doing great. Busy as we've ever been!"

I came clean and said "Robbie, you look light, there's no materials anywhere." And that's when Robbie shared a pretty amazing story about engaging with suppliers.

He told me how he set up meetings with his current material supplier and three perspective suppliers. He explained the specific challenges he was facing regarding material – a shortage of space, downward pricing pressure, and capacity limitations with some of his cutting equipment.. He engaged them in helping to develop solutions that could have positive impact on both of their businesses. Instead of beating them up for lower prices, he invited them to engage and partner.

One of the suppliers – who really wanted Robbie's large volumes – offered up the following solution: Place your order by noon, and we will have everything delivered by 8:00 AM the following day, cut to size and ready to print. In addition, they pledged to meet his current pricing.

The result? In very short order, Robbie was able to eliminate tens of thousands of dollars' worth of inventory. Next, he was able to reclaim a big chunk of his storage space and turn it into manufacturing space. In addition, he was able to speed up production by eliminating the very time-consuming cutting stage. All in all, this transformed Robbie's company – without even increasing his material cost! Bottom line, the supplier saved Robbie a TON of money and helped him deal with some major challenges. That's the power of real engagement.

As you consider your own issues and problems, I strongly encourage you to turn to your suppliers – material, supplies, hardware, software or whatever. Give them the chance to help you.

Here's a thought. If your suppliers read this book before you do, they may be encouraged to change their own approach to selling to you, seeking a more engaged and less transactional relationship. If they don't read the book, no problem! You can be the driver by engaging with – not just buying from – them.

14 Adding To Your Team
Brian Adam

I think I've made it pretty clear that I believe in *team*. Obviously, I'm not the only one. I did a Google search on "books on team building" and the result scrolled 51 titles across the top of the page – and I think that was only scratching the surface! So lots of us are writing about *building* teams, but I'm not sure enough of us are writing about the specific challenges of *adding* to an established team.

Tell me if this sounds familiar. You post a job, and a potential candidate applies for it, with a great resume, solid work history and glowing recommendations. Then he or she aces the interview, and joins the company, full of promise. It seems like a slam dunk, a perfect fit. Yet this individual is not successful, not engaged, not happy – just plain "not a fit." What happened? How do some individuals seem to fit in so well and instantly become engaged, while others don't fit in at all?

In my experience, it comes down to fitting with the company's culture. If an individual's internal motivations, drivers and values are not aligned with the culture of the organization, no amount of experience or education can make up for that culture gap. There is a high correlation between cultural fit and engagement. If an employee's values are aligned – if they feel like they can add value and fit in – they will very likely be a highly engaged, effective employee and a great hire.

So what does a poor culture fit look like? Let's think about some extreme (and hopefully humorous) examples:

- Mother Theresa working for a New York City Hedge Fund
- Snoop Dogg at the American Lung Association
- Mahatma Gandhi selling vacation time shares

- John Muir working for ExxonMobil
- Joel Osteen publishing Playboy
- Rosie O' Donnell working for Jenny Craig
- Michael Jordan playing minor league baseball – oh wait, that actually happened!

These individuals were all extremely successful in their own walks of life, and left a lasting impact on society. However, none of them would have been "a fit" for any of the organizations I placed them in. Had they worked for these organizations, they all likely would have failed, as their values and motivations would have been misaligned.

It Matters!

Cultural fit matters. If someone lacks the skills you can train them. If they don't fit your corporate culture, there's not much you can do about it. Here's the scary thing, cultural fit is too rarely at the top of the list, or even anywhere near top-of-mind when an organization is conducting a job search or going through the interview process.

Let's take a look at a typical job posting and how it demonstrates this misalignment:

> **Now Hiring!**
> **Experienced Account Manager**
> **Requirements:**
>
> - 5+ years of experience
> - Bachelor's degree or equivalent
> - Industry experience a plus
> - Microsoft excel proficiency
> - Hard-working, self-motivated, team player

From my perspective, this posting *disqualifies* a whole bunch of potential candidates – perhaps less educated or less experienced, but still potential superstars – who may also have been a great cultural fit for the role and the organization. Sure, the remaining candidates may check all the boxes for experience and background, but may not check *any* of the cultural fit boxes and might be misaligned with your core values.

Now, let's rewrite that job posting for cultural fit, using Olympus as an example, specifically for the type of Account Manager that fits our culture.

Account Manager – Cool projects. Big customers. Crazy fast deadlines!
Requirements:

- Responsiveness – Do you like to move FAST. We service the tradeshow and event industry. Things change quickly. No two days are alike.
- Team player – Do you thrive on individual accomplishments? If so, we're probably not a great fit. We work and win as a team, sharing accolades and success.
- Superstars win – We value, promote and reward performance over seniority. Want to move up and advance fast? If you're successful here, there are plenty of opportunities for advancement.
- Integrity – Would you give the shirt off your back to your neighbor, or a co-worker? If so, you'll fit in great here.

I think this posting paints a more accurate picture of our organization, and what it takes to thrive in our environment. It will therefore – hopefully! – attract candidates who fit our culture.

College Degree?

To me, cultural fit is far more important than experience or educational background. Give me a hard-working, high-integrity individual, with a sense of urgency. I'll take that any day over a 4.0 GPA. Some of the most successful employees at Olympus – including some of our leaders – do not have a college degree. In fact, I honestly have no idea who at Olympus has a college or advanced degree, and who does not. I do know that all of our successful leaders embrace, live and believe in our core values. Simply put, they are a cultural fit.

So why do most companies stress experience and education as qualifiers in the interviewing process? Mostly, I think, because they are easy to quantify. It's a lot easier to determine how many years someone has worked, or what their degree is in, than to determine if they are a cultural fit. Think about Olympus' core values:

- Selflessness
- "Can Do" Attitudes
- Gets Results
- Integrity

How do you quantify *those* attributes to determine if a potential candidate is a fit? It's not easy – which, again, is probably why most companies fall back to years of experience and education. But it is possible. We have found the most effective way to determine cultural fit is to ask a series of open-ended questions. I'll list some of those in a moment. First, though, let's break the overall hiring process down into two steps:

1. The Recruiting Process: How do you *attract* candidates who will be a cultural fit?
2. The Interview Process: How do you *select* candidates who will be a cultural fit? And, of equal importance, how do you *articulate* your culture to these candidates, so *they* can determine if you are a cultural fit for them?

The Recruiting Process

I believe that the primary goal of the recruiting process should be to cast the widest net possible. Get as many potential candidates into your process as you can, and then filter. I'd much rather start with 500 candidates than with 10, the sheer number increases the likelihood that we will find the best cultural fit.

At Olympus, we've made a significant investment in *establishing* our culture online. We're on LinkedIn and Facebook and in a wide range of industry associations and publications. We celebrate promotions, blog about cool projects, announce and introduce new hires. We communicate often and openly about our company and our culture. Heck, I'm even writing this book as part of that process, to share my feelings about our team with the world. We want our peers – and everyone else! – to know what's best about Olympus, and that's our culture, *plus* the cool things we are doing. We want people to read about us and think, *Hey, I'd like to work there!*

Once we post a job, I want it to reach as many people as possible. To accomplish that, we use job posting sites, social media sites, trade associations, local networks and recruiters. But one of the most effective methods has been our current team members. We post all jobs internally first, in our lunchrooms, on our wiki sites and our message boards. We also ask team members directly if they might know anyone who is a good fit. We offer referral bonuses – for both interviews and hires. Our belief is that a current employee who *is* a cultural fit will be likely to recommend individuals *they too* believe would fit in at Olympus, and some of our best hires have been recommend to us by our current team members.

As noted, we want to *fill* the funnel. Once that's been done, it's time to begin the interview process, and to start selecting the candidate who best fits our culture.

The Interview Process

I wonder if anyone's thinking that *too many* resumes can be a problem. Sure, it takes time to filter through them, and that can seem overwhelming. Our solution has been to ask the candidates to do some of the work.

We ask every applicant to complete a questionnaire as part of the application process. It's not overly difficult or arduous. We stick to some pretty basic questions:

- Tell us why you are interested in working for Olympus.
- How would you describe your ideal role?
- Tell us a bit about yourself.
- What made you successful in your previous role?

We have found this questionnaire to be a great filter. The answers provide a lot more insight about a candidate than the experience and education "facts" listed on their resumes. Starting with, *can the person communicate effectively in writing?* We probably disqualify half of all candidates because of spelling errors or incomplete answers. Think about that. Would you really want to hire someone who wasn't willing – or able – to check and double-check their work, or who wouldn't put in the time to complete the questionnaire? We need people who are willing to go above and beyond. That's what it takes to fit our culture. If you can't even – or won't even – spell-check your application, that's not a good sign! On the other hand, a series of thoughtful and complete answers is a very good sign.

The first four questions on our questionnaire are identified as mandatory. But we ask one more question, and we state that it's optional: *Please share your thoughts on why you would be a great fit at Olympus?* OK, it's optional, but not really. What it really is is still another part of the test, because if someone is not willing to go above and beyond to answer that one "optional" question when applying for a job, they likely won't fit our culture. We are constantly pushing ourselves to go above and beyond for our customers. If you don't answer that question, that's where the interview process ends.

If you do answer *all* of the questions – and, of course, if we like your answers! – the next stage is to bring you in for a face-to-face conversation. That typically starts with the hiring manager (your future boss), but it will also include HR, at least one member of our executive team, and some of the people you would be working alongside. We know that the peer part of the process is very important. On one hand, it gives the candidate another level of insight into the organization. In addition, it's another example of how we engage with our current team members. Remember, this is about *adding* to our team, and it's only *our* team if the players are represented in the decision.

Conversation

We are very clear with each candidate that this is meant to be a *conversation*. We're interviewing them, but we want them to interview us as well. We are hoping to be questioned about our culture, our expectations, our plans and their role. And we're honest with them. We're eager to talk about our strengths, and where we excel, but we're also willing to talk about our weaknesses and where we need to improve. Our rule is, don't oversell the job or the organization. We've learned that doesn't do anyone any good!

We also like to add "likely scenarios" into the interview process. With a salesperson, for example, we might describe a scenario which required some tradeoff between speed and quality, or a situation where closing the deal might stretch someone's integrity. With an engineer, we might describe a mechanical or workflow problem. *"How would you handle this"* We've found the answers are often very illuminating. As a general statement, we've found that anything you can do to put the candidate into the actual role they're being considered for – even hypothetically – will probably help you make a better hiring decision.

My Role

Whenever it's possible, I also meet and personally interview each individual. I do that knowing that I usually don't know how to do the job they're being considered for. Truthfully, I'm a poor judge of *talent* for 95% of the positions at Olympus. But that doesn't matter, because my part of the interview process is strictly focused on culture. I'll spend some time articulating our corporate culture – the good, the bad, the expectations. I try to articulate the ethos of who Olympus is and what we are trying to achieve. Then I ask a series of questions to help gauge cultural fit.

- Why do you want to work for our company?
- How would you describe the culture at previous companies you've worked at?
- Did you enjoy working in that company culture?
- What does a healthy work culture mean to you?
- How do you like to be managed?
- What does a perfect day look like for you?
- Aside from work, what are you passionate about?
- What's the last book you read?

After all of this, we compare notes. Cultural fit is a straight yes or no decision. If it's *yes*, we consider skills, knowledge and experience. If the training challenge seems reasonable, we're *almost* ready to offer the job.

Final Stage

The last step in our interview process is a background/reference check. But we do this differently than many companies. We don't want to follow-up or talk with references that the candidate provided. Those individuals will almost assuredly provide glowing recommendations. Instead, we dig and find references on our own. We have found this feedback to be extremely insightful. It sometimes confirms our own findings and feelings about skills, experience and character. It sometimes waves a warning flag, and I'm pretty sure that this stage alone has helped us to avoid some hiring mistakes.

This all takes time and effort, but I strongly believe that finding the best cultural fit is more than worth that investment. If the result is an engaged team member, you have just hit the jackpot!

Hey Dave, do you have any thoughts on this topic?

****

Yes, Brian, I do, starting with the fact that I love the idea that every interview should be a conversation. The Gold Standard in recruiting is for you to make a good hiring decision and them to make a good career decision. Classic win-win!

I'd also like to add a few things to the "requirements" you listed for Account Managers. I wouldn't necessarily put these in the job posting, but I'm always looking for four personality traits in a salesperson:

- Ego drive
- Assertiveness
- Empathy
- Dollar drive

I've learned that *ego drive* sounds bad to many people. Really, the last thing most people want is to have to deal with a salesperson with a huge ego! But that's not what the term means. *Drive* is the key word, not *ego*. Think of it this way, some people get their joy from convincing other people to agree with them. They relish the challenge of changing peoples' minds. And, at a fundamental level, that's what sales is often all about. One of the principles I teach is that most times the main competition is the *status quo*, in other words, whatever way whoever you're trying to sell to has been doing whatever it is that relates to your product or service. That might be another product, or another supplier, or the fact that's it's just something they've never done before. Whatever, some *convincing* will be required.

Assertiveness is the willingness to push a little bit to be convincing. Not too much! I would call that *aggressiveness*, and that's a bad thing. But I do want someone who's willing to stand up for their product or service or company, who won't be derailed by the first obstacle or objection.

Empathy is the ability to put yourself into another person's head, or heart – in other words, to understand their perspective. *Dollar drive* is sort of like being motivated by money. I say sort of, because I don't think anyone is truly motivated by money. I personally have always been motivated by *what I could do* with money. A few examples: driving a nice car, living in a nice house, going to nice restaurants and donating to worthy causes. I've been motivated to work hard in order to earn the money that would let me do these things. I think you'll agree that most salespeople – certainly commission salespeople – have more opportunity to increase their earnings than most other wage-earners. All I'm really saying is that I look for salespeople who will take advantage of that opportunity.

Interview and Testing

So, how do you identify those personality traits? You can test for three of them, but let me come back to that in a moment. You can also interview for them, and here's how I do that.

"I am looking for a salesperson who has *ego drive*," I say, as part of the interview conversation. "Do you know what that means?"

No is an acceptable answer to that question. If that's the answer, I explain, and then we move on from there. *Yes*, all by itself, is a dangerous answer – for the candidate! – because I will then say, "OK, please tell me what it means." Whether we call it an interview or a conversation, this is a test. As Brian noted, failing to answer the "optional" question on Olympus's questionnaire results in immediate disqualification. So should trying to bullshit the interviewer, especially for a sales position.

If we get past that stage, here's where I take the conversation: "Please tell me a story that indicates that you have the ego drive I'm looking for." Then

I'll do the very same thing with assertiveness, empathy and dollar drive.

Back to the testing. I use a profile called Caliper as the last stage of my process for hiring a salesperson. *Ego drive*, in fact, is Caliper terminology. The Caliper Profile also quantifies assertiveness and empathy, along with numerous other personality traits. It's the last stage because there's a cost involved, and it's more than I'd want to spend for a "screening" tool, but I think it's a very reasonable investment once you've gotten to the point where you're otherwise convinced that you have a winner. Caliper has application to other-than-sales positions too. You can learn more at www.calipercorp.com.

Teams In General

Like Brian, I'm a strong believer in *team*. Let's talk a little bit about teams and teamwork in general, though. Here's something that Peter Drucker wrote in a 1992 article in the Wall Street Journal: "'Team building' has become a buzzword in American business. The results are not overly impressive."

You might be surprised that I'm quoting Drucker here when what he said is so negative, but he went on to explain his perception of the problem, "the all-but-universal belief among executives that there is just one kind of team. There actually are three – each different in its structure, in the behavior it demands from its members, in its strengths, its vulnerabilities, its limitations, its requirements, but above all, in what it can do and should be used for."

The first kind of team, according to Drucker, is the baseball team, which he also compared to an assembly line. The players play on the team; they do not play as a team. They have fixed positions they never leave.

The second kind of team is the football team, which he also compared to a symphony orchestra. The players still have fixed positions, but they support each other and interact with each other to a far greater degree. The receiver runs a pass pattern, the left tackle protects the quarterback's blind side, the quarterback makes the throw, and the result is (hopefully) a completed pass. The horn section plays a sequence of notes, the string section plays another sequence of notes, the conductor manages the timing, and the result is (hopefully) music to our ears.

The third kind of team is the tennis doubles team, which Drucker compared to a jazz combo. Here, the players have a primary position rather than a fixed one. In doubles tennis, when one player serves, the other takes a position to cover a part of the court when the serve is returned, but once the play starts, both players must be able to react to the changing demands of the game. In jazz, the players are encouraged to take turns in a musical game of follow the leader – to keep up when it's their turn to follow, and to take the music to another level when it's their turn to lead.

Lessons To Learn

What can we take from all of this? First, let's understand that a baseball team is a limited model for a business team (with one caveat, that I'll get to in a moment.) Second, let's consider that a football team is as dependent on its coach as it is on its players. Someone has to draw the play. Someone has to call the play. Without the play – the plan! – a football team is a collection of mass and energy without direction, which is not a recipe for success.

Third, let's recognize that a tennis doubles team requires a level of collaboration that goes beyond running a play or playing a musical score. I think it's significant that doubles teammates usually refer to each other as *partner*. There's more to it than a shared commitment to winning, though, even baseball teams have that. Maybe I can explain it this way. There's an element of *anticipation* in great doubles play, knowing what your partner is likely to do, and moving into position to support that play before it actually happens. In management, it's more a matter of understanding, knowing what your teammate would want or need out of any given situation, and incorporating that knowledge into your response to the situation.

Here's an example. One of my clients is a manufacturing company, and one of their machines broke down, threatening a delivery commitment. The Production Manager at this company knew that he had three options. One, he could call for normal repair service, which would probably have the machine running again the next day, but would result in an unhappy customer. Two, he could call for rush service, which would probably have the machine running in time to avoid any consequences with the customer, but the rush repair charges would also eat most of the profit on that particular order. Three, he could outsource the work, but that would eat all of the profit on the order, and then some.

He decided to call for normal service. Because he also knew two other things. One, the customer in question was a bad customer. (As I hope you'll remember, I define a bad customer as one who's more trouble than they're worth. This customer certainly was, contributing a fair amount of volume, but not a lot of profit, and causing lots of disruption with their often unreasonable demands.) Two, his company was in a dispute with the only company he could have outsourced the work to. Sending them a rush order would have given them leverage in that dispute.

So, even though the decision to call for normal service would result in an unhappy customer, the "bigger-picture" considerations made it the right decision. The owner of the company was very pleased with the way his Production Manager handled this situation. They worked well as a team, without a whole lot of visible teamwork. But it probably took a lot of work to build the team!

Your Team(s)

Please also note that team(s) can be plural, and they can be different types of teams in play, all at the same time. It's also worth noting that an individual can be a member of some teams and the manager/leader of others.

The Production Manager I just mentioned is a perfect example. He's a member of a tennis-doubles-type team with his boss – not the leader, but definitely a partner. He does lead the production team, and part of the way he does that is by putting the production plan together every day – the "game plan" by which a wide range of projects move through the various parts of the company's production process. Another way he does that is by anticipating problems, and coaching his players on how to avoid them, and how to respond to them if they can't be avoided. He would tell you, I think, that his production team is mostly a football-type team, with some baseball-type team situations, and some tennis-doubles-type team opportunities. He would also tell you, I think, that the best way to manage is to make everyone a manager.

Here's what that means. The lowest ranking employee at this company is a young man who does finishing work and makes deliveries. Sometimes the work involves machines, but more often it's handwork. He probably spends half of his other-than-delivery time putting odd-sized parts and products into packages.

He works under the direction and supervision of the Production Manager, but once he's given an assignment, he becomes directly responsible for managing something. He doesn't manage other people, but let's understand that management can involve any combination of people, projects, products and/or processes. The key point here is that if this young man is properly trained – and fully engaged! – he can manage a project or a process with a minimum of supervision. He can make sure that everything from the big things to the little things — within that project or process — gets done and done right. And by doing so, he can be a very valuable part of the management team.

In this case, it's a baseball-model team, and that takes us back to something I mentioned earlier – that a baseball team is a limited model for a management team, with one caveat. The caveat is that you want every player on a baseball team to be competent (at the very least) at his or her position. If any skills are lacking, you have only two options. One is to train them in to the player you have. The only other reasonable option is to replace the player with someone who does have those skills. And remember, it's not just skills, it's also attitudes and cultural fit.

Macro vs. Micro

Here's a final thought on your team(s). The people who run the government talk a lot about creating jobs. In the "macro" sense, they're talking about creating new jobs, to bring unemployment down. What I'd like you to think about is a "micro" opportunity – where you create a job by releasing the person who's currently doing it. That won't provide a net gain for the economy, but it could be a significant gain for your company.

If there's an upside to high unemployment, it's that talented and productive people are looking for jobs, and among the unemployed and underemployed right now are thousands of disciplined and dedicated individuals who have very recently served their country, people who come from a culture of training and professionalism. Doesn't that describe a lot of what you want in a member of your team? I hope you'll consider hiring a vet the next time you have –- or create – an open position.

But whoever your next hire is, I hope you'll give some thought to the best possible onboarding process. Let me give the ball back to Brian for his thoughts on that issue.

****

Thanks, Dave. OK, you've hired a person who seems to be a good cultural fit. You have to understand, though, you do not yet have a *fully engaged* employee. *Onboarding* is the next step toward *engagement*. Let's think about the way most companies onboard new employees. Sadly, a typical new employee's first day tends to look something like this:

- New Employee shows up, and no one is there to greet them. The receptionist has no idea who they are, and pages HR.
- HR shows up eventually. New Employee then sits in corner filling out HR paperwork.
- New Employee's new boss is too busy to talk that day. New Employee is sent off to shadow co-workers, who are busy with their own jobs
- Lunch time. New Employee goes out to lunch, probably alone
- Through the afternoon, New Employee fills out more paperwork, continues to shadow co-workers.
- At some point, HR provides a tour, including emergency exits, eye wash station and where to take shelter in a tornado.
- All too often, New Employee's workspace is not ready. No desk, no phone, no computer, no business cards, etc.
- All too often, no one really engages with the new kid. At the end of the day, New Employee still feels like a Stranger In A Strange Land.
- New Employee goes home feeling uninspired, and possibly feeling some regret about the decision to come work at this place.
- Day 2: If it doesn't get better, it can only get worse!

OK, that's a worst case scenario. But if your onboarding scenario is even remotely similar, you'll miss a golden opportunity to make a *really* good first impression and you will have failed the first stage of employee engagement. This is really not that different from walking into a store and getting the cold shoulder from a retail clerk. If the onboarding process feels *transactional*, it's just like a sales clerk who simply rings up an order and places the purchased goods in a bag or box.

And think about this, we're talking about someone you may have spent considerable time searching for, and interviewing, and someone in whom you'll make a significant investment in training. Aren't we talking about someone you hope will grow with your company, for years to come, and someone whom you hope will demonstrate high levels of engagement in their role every day? Don't think of onboarding as the last stage of the hiring process. It is *absolutely* the first stage of the engagement process.

No, wait, it's the *next* step of the engagement process, which really started during the interviewing stage. You see that, right?

A Better Day

So, what might a better Day 1 look like? How would you feel if you were the New Employee and when you walked in your first day went more like this:

- Your manager is waiting for you and actually greets you at the door.
- Your manager takes you to your new workspace, which is set up and fully functional – everything you will need to do your job.
- Your new business cards are there too, along with a small gift for you to take home to your family, and a handwritten note from your manager to your family, thanking them for their part in your joining the team.
- Your manager takes you for a comprehensive tour of the facility, and introduces you to every possible team member. (It's worth noting that we set a special start time for a new employee's first day. Our normal start time is 8:00 AM, but we ask each new employee to arrive at 8:30 – just to give ourselves a little extra time to make all of this happen!)
- The President personally welcomes you to the team, meeting one-on-one with you, sharing the company history and an overview of the company culture. The President asks you about your family, and what you do for fun outside of work.
- Your new co-workers take you out to lunch on the company's dime.
- Day 2: Your manager meets with you, first thing, with two questions: "How was your first day? What else can we do to help you get comfortable and fully up to speed?"

Now, it will no doubt take some work to make all of this happen. But the question is, will that work – that *investment* in time and effort – be worthwhile? Will this *engagement-based onboarding strategy* result in a more engaged employee?

You know the answer, don't you? Because I asked you to think about how *you* would feel if your first day went like this. As noted earlier, part of my goal in writing this is to share some of the "tips and tricks" I've learned about Employee Engagement. I frequently ask myself: *"How would I feel if I was on the receiving end of whatever action or policy or procedure is being considered."* That doesn't always change my decision, but it's part of the decision-making process, and if nothing else, it help me prepare for possible ramifications.

15 Case Study: Carolina Ballet
Dave Fellman

I mentioned earlier that my wife is a classically trained ballerina. She has long since retired as a performer, but she continues to take class on a pretty regular basis. (It may be worth noting that dancers take "class" to work on their skills. Those who perform go to "rehearsals" to apply those skills to a specific piece of choreography, to get ready to perform it. It would be common for a professional to take class in the morning, then go to rehearsal in the afternoon, with a performance in the evening.)

Anyway, my wife takes class these days at The School of the Carolina Ballet. On any given day, there might be classes for Adult Beginner and Adult Intermediate levels along with 8-10 classes for children at various stages and levels, and 2-3 Company Classes for the company's performers. The School has four studios, and at peak times, they're all in use, with classes running back-to-back-to-back.

The studio area has a particular rhythm. About ten minutes before each class starts, the dancers start assembling in the hallway. The older, more experienced dancers usually sit and stretch. The younger students mostly sit and chatter. The mothers and occasional fathers who are picking up or dropping off stand off to the side. At the designated time, the studio doors open, and people start moving out and moving in. Within just a few minutes, the hallway is empty again, until ten-or-so minutes before the next classes.

This is how it works, no matter where you go in ballet, and it's probably the same at gymnastics and karate schools too. But my wife tells me that there's something unique about The School of the Carolina Ballet, something she's never encountered before.

Recently she told me about seeing the company's Artistic Director engage with a group of "baby ballerinas" in the hallway – tiny little 5-6 year old girls in pink tutus. He asked them if they knew how to do the "truffle shuffle." (*Truffle* is one of those "little kid" roles I mentioned earlier in The Nutcracker.) He demonstrated the steps, then he tapped fingers and bumped fists with most of the little girls. Then he continued tapping fingers and bumping fists with the 10-or-so mothers in the hallway.

"You *never* see that," my wife told me. "Artistic directors? Their usual attitude is 'get these annoying little children – and their annoying mothers! – away from my studio!'"

The company dancers also engage regularly with other students – both children and adults. As I understand it, company members tend to be somewhat aloof. They are, after all, at work when they're in the studio, while just about everyone else is there for recreational classes. But at The School of the Carolina Ballet, they tend to smile and make eye contact and even start conversations on their way in and out of class. Because it's so rare to her experience, my wife speculates that someone told them to do it.

I'd be willing to bet that someone did tell them, although *tell* would not be my word of preference. I want to think that someone *asked* them to *engage with their customers*. And that – the *customer* part – is an important understanding.

It's A Business

Your business is all about selling something to somebody. As I hope you'll remember, I wrote those words all the way back in the introduction. And by definition, anyone who buys from you is a customer, right? So let's talk a little bit about this "ballet business" and its customers.

Carolina Ballet is what I refer to as an *artistic non-profit*. Approximately half of its funding comes from donations and grants, and that part of the business is the responsibility of a six-person sales team. Now, they probably don't call themselves a sales team, and all of their titles include the words *gift* or *development* as opposed to *sales*, but make no mistake, their job is to sell the idea of supporting Carolina Ballet, through personal or corporate donations or the assignment of grant money. And make no mistake about this too, someone else wants every penny of that money! Carolina Ballet's fundraisers are in competition every day, with a wide range of other artistic and charitable non-profits. It is fundamentally no different than the competition between retail stores, restaurants, fitness clubs, landscape contractors, printing companies or anyone else.

The *development* revenue stream is augmented by the *performance* revenue stream. This part of the business is the responsibility of three people who make up the Marketing & Communications team, and seventeen more whose titles actually do say *sales*. The Marketers include a Director, a Coordinator and a Graphic/Web Designer. They own the advertising and all other Marketing Communication. The Sales Team includes a Director and sixteen sales associates, whose job is to sell tickets, both individually and by subscription.

I have developed something of a relationship with one of the sales associates. Her name is Megan, and she has what I think of as one of the better variants of the worst job in the world.

What does that mean? We all hate telemarketers, right? Even those of us who sell on the phone tend to hate the telemarketing calls we receive – especially the ones that come in the evening when we're trying to relax. But even though I hate the calls, I try not to hate the callers. I believe in Sales Karma. If I treat another salesperson badly, I lose at least some of the right to complain when I'm treated badly myself. So I try to be pleasant when I'm on the receiving end of a sales or fundraising call, even in the evening. But I make it clear if I'm not interested. Day or night, I will often say: "I'm not a very good prospect for what you sell, and I'd like to be taken off your list." With fundraising calls, I often say: "I know it's a good cause, but I'm sorry, I can't help you today."

I will say this, if the salesperson just continues blasting on with his/her script, I usually hang up. And I hang up immediately on robocalls.

Target List

Back to Megan, and her "better variant." If I were in charge of building the ticket sales database for the Carolina Ballet sales team, I would start with everyone who has even been a customer – in other words, everyone who has ever attended a performance *and* everyone who has ever taken a class at the ballet school. I would then add everyone who has ever donated to the company. That's a pretty significant database of people who have some demonstrated interest in "the product," wouldn't you agree? So those are not *cold calls*, in fact, they're *customer maximization* calls.

To add to the database, I would consider the *demographics* of the initial list. What kind of people go to the ballet? The first word that comes to mind is *prosperous*. Another is *educated*. Still another is *upscale*. So now I'm thinking that, if I start calling *everyone* who lives within, say, a thirty-mile radius of the venue where Carolina Ballet performs, I'm going to generate a lot of hate. (It's my theory that the amount of hate generated by a telemarketing call is inversely related to the level of interest that the call recipient may possess. High interest tends toward low hate. Low interest tends toward high hate. Makes sense, right?)

So instead of calling *everyone*, I'm going to develop a target list of people who fit into the *prosperous/educated/upscale* category, and there's plenty of data available to help me do that. (The truth is, it's scary how much data is out there. Facebook and Google know a lot about you – read that: **A LOT ABOUT YOU!** – and there are many other resources available to help you find the data you want/need.)

The point is that Megan gets to call on people who are, at the very least, *likely suspects*. Many of them are actual customers. They're not all going to buy tickets from her, but they're also not all going to hang up on her, or hate the call (or the caller) in the first place.

Skill and Professionalism

My relationship with Megan has its roots in her skill and professionalism. I have *never* felt like she was reading off a script. I have *always* felt like she was helping us to make the decision to buy from her. The first time she called, I was at home alone. She asked for my wife, by name. I said: "She's not here. May I ask who's calling?" She said: "My name is Megan (plus her last name). I'm calling from the Carolina Ballet." I said: "That's a coincidence, she's out at ballet class right now."

Megan asked where, and I told her. This was quite a few years ago, and actually before Carolina Ballet opened its own public school. But Megan recognized the name of the other school and made a positive comment about their program. Then she told me the reason for her call: "I have Mrs. Fellman on my list of regular attendees, and I'm calling to offer her a special subscription rate for our upcoming season. Is that something I can talk to you about, or do I need to talk to her?"

I said: "That sounds like a good deal, but she's the one you'll have to talk to. She'll be home in an hour or so, if you'd like to call then."

"I'll do that," she said, and sure enough, an hour or so later, the phone rang again. My wife answered this time, and had what sounded like a very pleasant conversation over the next 10-15 minutes. I could only hear our side of the conversation, but it was apparent that Megan was asking about her class that evening, and her overall ballet experience. In other words, she was *engaging* with her customer.

The conversation ended with my wife committing to call her "ballet peeps," to see if any of them wanted in on the special offer, and Megan committing to call again later in the week. And when she called, guess what, I was home alone again.

"Hello, Mr. Fellman," she said. "This is Megan (plus her last name) from the Carolina Ballet. I had promised to get back with Mrs. Fellman tonight. Is she in?"

"Nope," I said. "Kick-boxing tonight. But she should be back any minute. Literally any minute. In the meantime, want to talk to me? I have something I want to ask you."

"Sure," she said – and I can only imagine what she thought was going to happen next. Possibly "OMG, this old man is going to hit on me!"

But that wasn't it. "I wanted to ask you if you like your job, being a telemarketer?"

Ambassador For A Really Great Company

She was silent for a couple of beats, then she said: "I don't think of myself as a telemarketer. I'm more of an ambassador for a really great company. What could be better than that?"

We talked about her job for a few more minutes, until my wife came home. Since then, we've probably talked 10-12 more times. Megan knows now what I do for a living, so she understands why I'm interested in her perspective on selling. I have asked her for horror stories about her worst calling experiences. She has told me some doozies! And she has also confirmed some of what I've surmised about the whole Carolina Ballet organization.

Yes, they have been asked to *engage with their customers*. Perhaps more importantly, they have been *trained* in how to do it. I haven't had any personal experience with the development team, but it's obvious to me that the other two revenue streams are living the mission. And the "business" seems healthy, so it would seem that the development team is equally engaged.

Here, by the way, is the mission statement:

Carolina Ballet's mission is to perform world-class professional ballet, entertaining and enlightening audiences in Raleigh, the Triangle region, the State of North Carolina, and beyond. It will accomplish this mission by:

- *attracting, developing, and retaining excellent dancers and artistic personnel combined with a fiscally responsible management and board of directors;*
- *commissioning new works by innovative choreographers;*
- *presenting traditional ballets of legendary masters;*
- *educating current and future audiences through programs for school-aged children and other performance outreach activities.*

I think the part Brian will like best is the part about *attracting, developing, and retaining excellent dancers and artistic personnel.* I know the part I like best is the part about *educating current and future audiences through programs for school-aged children and other performance outreach activities.* I'm not sure either of us loves the rest of it. Too "boilerplate" maybe? But let's consider the long-term vision. Carolina Ballet is consciously engaging with both current and future customers *and* team-members. Pretty good strategy, right?

OK, you may never go to the ballet. But I hope you'll appreciate that it's a business. It has some unique challenges, but also some that are probably pretty similar to your own. From my perspective, it's a good example of *engagement* on numerous levels. And I'm wondering, are there ways you can apply some of their strategies to your business?

16 Engagement During A Pandemic
Brian Adam

During the spring of 2020, while Dave and I were in the middle of writing this book, Covid-19 hit, impacting and changing the world, seemingly overnight. The Covid pandemic created massive humanitarian challenges: millions sick, hundreds of thousands of lost lives, soaring unemployment. Economies were shut down, just about everyone stopped traveling, and at Olympus, most of our major markets shut down hard. Our largest customers and biggest markets are tradeshows and events, sports teams and amusement parks. Each of these markets is contingent on large groups of people gathering together in one place at the same time, something that just wasn't viable in a Covid world. Within the span of one week, we went from discussing expansion plans and major, multi-million dollar investments in new printing equipment to wondering if the company was going to survive. There was no doubt, this pandemic was an existential threat to our business, a complete shock that rocked our world.

This book is about the *Rules of Engagement*, and some of them have obviously changed. I personally have learned some valuable lessons during this pandemic, which instantly changed how our employees work, how our customers behave, how our supply chains operate and what our goals are. We still don't know when – or even if! – tradeshows, amusement parks, sports teams and other events will return to pre-Covid levels. As I'm writing this, Covid-19 is still around and a very real threat.

But having said that, I feel that our focus on *engagement* and our overall culture have played a key role in helping position us to survive this threat. I now believe that Olympus Group is well-positioned to capitalize on the economic rebound when it occurs. We are no longer talking about *if* Olympus will survive, but rather *what we want to look like* coming out of this crisis.

Before sharing our takeaways and what we learned, though, I'd like to share a bit about Olympus' Covid story.

Early 2020

As we started the new year, Covid-19 seemed like an issue on the other side of the world. Wuhan, China, where it all started, was a place I knew nothing about. I assumed, ignorantly as it turned out, that our company and our business would not be impacted.

The new year was off to a good start. We had onboarded some new, high potential customers. The sales pipeline was full, and as a sports fan, born & raised in Wisconsin, it was a dream year. The Bucks were having their greatest season ever, and were the favorites to win the NBA championship. The Brewers resigned Christian Yelich, arguably the best player in baseball. The Packers would return most of their starters from a team that reached the NFC championship game. The Badgers basketball team won 8 games in a row, to win a share of the Big Ten title heading into the NCAA tournament. As a large format printer serving the sports market, we were feeling very fortunate. Local sports teams' success often translates into a lot of print work for us.

The city of Milwaukee was set to have a banner year (pun intended). In addition to the sports success, the Democratic National Convention was scheduled to come to Milwaukee in the summer of 2020, and our team was actively working on a number of large printing projects to support the event. The city of Milwaukee had an energy about it that I never felt before.

At our other locations, it was the same story. Our Denver team was posting record revenues. Gaylord had opened a 500,000 square foot event center out near Denver International Airport, with a full schedule of tradeshows, and our team was busy. In Orlando, Universal Studios was working on a massive expansion project as they opened a new theme park called Epic Universe. Orlando's tradeshow & event schedule was full, and our team was busy. We were feeling great about our momentum and very optimistic about our future.

And then, the second week of March, our world imploded. In the span of a week, the NBA suspended their season, the NCAA cancelled the Final Four, Major League Baseball stopped all spring training games, numerous tradeshows and events were postponed and Walt Disney World and Universal Studios shut down.

I still clearly remember the eerie morning when the reality of the situation hit me. It was Monday, March 16. Our executive team held a planned, quarterly off-site meeting. We had a room reserved at the local Hilton Garden Inn – the same meeting room we've met in every quarter over the past two year. As I pulled into the parking lot at 7:45 AM, everything was quiet – really quiet! – and empty. The hotel has 150 rooms, and the parking lot is usually packed. On this morning, there were less than ten cars in the parking lot and half of them belonged to my co-workers. As I walked into our meeting room, our facilitator and Olympus Board Member, Fred Pockrandt, mentioned that he had stayed at the hotel the previous evening. At check-in, they told him he was likely to be the only guest. As an accountant, numbers started spinning through my head. One guest, in a hotel with 150 rooms, no one in the restaurant. This is not good for business. Things could get ugly!

The Next Stage

Three days later, I got a call from one of my college roommates, Mike Stadler. Mike was the smart/driven one in our six-person apartment. He's a hard-working, high character guy, who is much smarter than I am. Mike went on to become an ENT surgeon, and had recently been promoted to Chief Medical Officer at Froedtert Hospital, the largest hospital in the Milwaukee area. The conversation went something like this:

> Mike – "Brian, you guys cut and sew things, right?"
> Me – "Sure. It's what we do every day"
> Mike – "We're getting desperate here, any chance you could make PPE?"
> Me – "PP-what?"
> Mike – "Personal Protective Equipment. Face masks & face shields"
> Me – "Mike, our markets are shut and work is drying up. We are desperate to keep our team working. We'll try anything",
> Mike – "Great! Let me make an introduction, you might be able to help"

That afternoon, Mike introduced us to Dr. Silvia Munoz-Price, the Director of the Division of Infectious Diseases at Froedtert Hospital. She explained their needs and asked if we could produce protective plastic face shields and cloth face masks. We had all sorts of questions about material specs, preferred construction methods, efficacy of products, FDA approvals, etc, etc. Dr. Munoz-Price's response to all of our questions was a consistent "something is better than nothing, we'll take what we can get."

We hustled back to our facility, scoured our shelves to determine what materials we had in stock, and within 24 hours, our team had engineered the products and set-up production lines. Neither of these products were overly technical – a couple of layers of fabric, a cut plastic shield with a headband. Froedtert didn't need anything rigorously engineered, what they needed was someone who could respond quickly. That's something we pride ourselves in. Within 72-hours of my call from Mike, the Olympus team delivered our first batch of several thousand face shields.

Never in my wildest dreams did I think we would be producing medical products, to be used by doctors and nurses to help protect them from a deadly virus during a global pandemic. We make banners and mascots, not medical products. Yet over the next couple of months we produced hundreds of thousands of face shields and face masks. This temporary work kept our team members busy, allowed us to avoid layoffs and helped us do a very, very small part in helping fight a pandemic.

All four of the states we have facilities in issued stay at home orders during the early stages of the pandemic, essentially shutting down all businesses and requiring all employees to stay at home, unless your business was deemed "essential." Since our team was manufacturing PPE, our Milwaukee, Orlando and Denver facilities all remained open and fully operational. The only real work we had in-house was PPE, but it allowed our team members to stay engaged and earn a paycheck.

Still. It was a scary time. As the crisis unfolded, we were scrambling. Every day it felt like something new was emerging. A customer was furloughing all of its employees. Another customer was closing its doors, probably permanently. New symptoms of the virus emerged, means of transmission changed, we were plunged into a world of uncertainty. But our team members were coming to work every day to produce PPE, even with the real risk of potential exposure to the virus.

Communication

As I've written, I have always believed in frequent and transparent communication with our team. Pre-Covid, I sent out weekly updates, published monthly newsletters and held quarterly town halls. In general, I always tried to *over-communicate*. With the pace of change, and the amount of uncertainty, we double-downed on those efforts. I began sending out company-wide updates twice a day – a morning and an evening update. These updates ranged widely: new products, what was happening to our customers, information on the virus as shared by the CDC, stories of our team members embodying our core values. Good news, bad news, it didn't matter, we shared it all.

My communication strategy became based around three important questions:

- What do we know?
- What do we not know?
- How you can help?

I believe it is important to be open about what is unknown – every bit as important as it is to share *known* facts and information. Admitting what you don't know helps employees be more empathetic to your response. I also encouraged our employees to provide feedback, ask questions and share their feelings. I repeatedly sent out my cell phone number to all 200+ employees, and encouraged them to call or text whenever they had a question or a concern. Personally connecting to our team members was paramount to ensuring that we maintained engagement throughout the crisis.

Remote Work

Like so many other companies during the pandemic, we faced the challenges of having people working remotely. It may have been a larger challenge for us, I think, because we're so focused on a fully engaged workforce. It wasn't just a matter of logistics, but also of engagement.

Some of our decisions were pretty straightforward. A core production role, like operating a digital printer, requires a person to physically be at our facility. Other roles, like sales for example, do not. So, we asked ourselves, do we require ALL employees to come to the office? Or do we treat our employees differently and allow certain roles to work from home? We did not want to expose our employees to unnecessarily risk in an effort to treat all employees equally, but we also did not want to disengage employees by creating two different standards.

Our COO, Jason Ahart, and our VP-Human Capital, Scott Coulthurst came up with a solution. They spoke with each employee, to better understand *their* individual situations, and then attempted to personalize a solution for each one.

For production employees who were not comfortable coming to the shop, we made exceptions and delivered materials to their homes. Mascots were being cut, sewn, glued, painted and fabricated at the homes of our team members. Seamstresses were getting weekly deliveries of material, and thousands of fabric face masks were being sewn. It wasn't perfect, and it certainly wasn't the most efficient model, but it allowed the team to stay engaged.

We also asked all of our executives and office personnel to sign up to work on the PPE production lines. We had more orders than we could handle, and took an "all hands on deck" approach to getting these face shields and face masks completed. Scott and Jason assigned me the task of attaching foam headbands to the face shields. Given my mechanical ineptness and lack of any real skills, I'm sure this was the easiest, most rudimentary part of the entire process. "Give Brian something he can't possibly screw up."

From an engagement perspective, it was HUGE. Our executives and office personnel spent their days with our hard-working production employees. I spent days on the production floor, dressed in a t-shirt, working side-by-side with our amazing team members. While my contributions to the finished products were negligible, the connections with team members certainly went a long, long way toward full employee engagement, both now and when we have Covid-19 behind us.

Focus On What You Can Control

Here's one more lesson learned. During the pandemic, there have been so many things that are outside of our control, at times I have felt helpless. I couldn't prevent tradeshows from being cancelled or postponed. I couldn't control whether the 2020 sports seasons were going to happen, I had no influence over when Disney and Universal Studios would reopen their theme parks. The spread of the virus, access to testing, vaccine development – all extremely important to me and the team at Olympus, but all outside my control.

I learned very early in the crisis to stop focusing on those things. Instead, I tried to focus on things that I *could* control. My messaging and communication to team members, what I spent my time working on, staying connected to key customers and suppliers, ensuring my employees' concerns were being addresses. Those I could impact and control, and that focus allowed us to align our efforts, and spend our resources on the things that mattered to us, regardless of how trivial.

Closing Story

By late March, we were in full production of PPE. We were printing, sewing and assembling thousands of masks and shields daily, but supply chains were still disrupted. It was extremely challenging to source even simple materials. Something as simple as elastic (which under normal circumstances was available in abundance) was in short supply. We were getting desperate. We had just received an order for 10,000 face masks for the Orlando Police Department. Great news – we were helping protect the professionals who were keeping Orlando safe. Only we had a major issue, we only had enough elastic to produce about 500 face masks.

We called our traditional suppliers and were quoted lead-times in *months* – when we needed this material in days, if not hours. There was no way such a long lead-time was going to cut it. We were desperate, and started reaching out to everyone that we thought might possibly have any elastic. We got a lead on some "ends" – thousands of yards of mixed lengths of elastic. The material we typically use comes neatly wound on rolls. You unroll it, cut off what you want, and use it. A box of mixed length elastic was going to add a lot of cost, given the labor required to sort, organize and cut it, but it bought us a little time, and we produced a few thousand face masks using the "ends."

But we still needed more, a lot more! Our purchasing team got another lead, but there was a catch. The only thing this supplier had in stock was "pink, lacy elastic." We didn't know exactly what that meant, but we were desperate so we placed the order. A couple of large boxes arrived on our dock the following day. As we opened the first box, we found the description to be completely accurate. It was pink, and boy was it lacy. We had just received a giant shipment of elastic that would normally be used in the production of ladies' lingerie.

We reached out to the Orlando Police Department and explained the situation.

> Olympus - "We can start shipping more face masks tomorrow, but there's a catch."
> Orlando PD - "Great news. What's the catch"
> Olympus – "Elastic is in short supply. The only elastic we have in stock and are able to source is pink, lacy elastic."
> Orlando PD – "Cool! Pink lacy elastic it is."

We started sewing right away, and shipped the order the next day. I like to think it makes a pretty good story/visual. *Orlando police officer apprehends bad guy while wearing a beautiful, pink, lacy elastic face mask!*

Albert Einstein famously said, "In the middle of difficulty, lies opportunity." I believe that, in midst of the Covid-19 crisis, many opportunities have and will continue to present themselves. Companies that remain connected to their team members, with high levels of engagement, will be the ones best positioned to survive and thrive through this crisis.

****

Maybe I can expand on that, to be the final words of this book:

Companies that are connected to their team members, their customers and their suppliers – that create and maintain high levels of engagement! – will always be the ones best positioned for long-term success.